Finding The Angels

A Personal Guide to Healing and Rediscovery After Divorce

By

Eric M. De Castro

Dedication

I'd like to dedicate this book to:

My parents (Aurea & Cesar)

My grandparents (Lucia & Lucio Manghinang) (Corazon & Mariano De Castro)

My extraordinary children (Zaquery, Dylan, and Ethan)

& My partner in crime and the love of my life, MKS

Table of Contents

Acknowledgement

They say it takes a village to raise a child. What a spectacular understatement. It takes a sprawling, messy, loyal, and sometimes unexpected tribe to rebuild a life, and an even bigger one to write a book about it. This isn't just a list of names; it's a debt of gratitude to the people who were the foundation and the architects of this new chapter.

This book is dedicated to the ones who came before, my original blueprint: my parents, Aurea & Cesar, and my grandparents, Lucia & Lucio Manghinang and Corazon & Mariano De Castro. You laid the foundation for a life I had to lovingly dismantle and rebuild. Thank you for the lessons, both the clear and the complicated.

To my extraordinary children, Zaquery, Dylan, and Ethan: You are my true north. Your resilience, your grace, and your willingness to let me remain a part of your lives is the greatest gift I have ever received.

And to MKS, my partner in crime and the love of my life. You are the steady hand in this second act, the one who proves that the best stories are the ones you don't see coming. My world is better for having you in it.

Then there are the others. The ones who answered the late-night phone calls, who sat in comfortable silence when words were useless, who listened without ever trying to fix a thing. You know who you are, and I dedicate this to all of you as well. You gave me the perseverance to see this through.

Finally, for every individual going through this hard period, I see you. You may not know this, but you helped me write this book. Your quiet fight, your questions, your resilience—that is the ink this story is written in.

Thank you all.

Forward

For many years, my life unfolded on a path that felt familiar and secure, a foundation built on the enduring examples set by those who came before me. I grew up witnessing the quiet strength and lasting commitment of my grandparents, who shared over fifty-five years of marriage, never once considering a different path. My parents, too, mirrored this steadfastness; their marriage also spanned more than fifty-five years, a testament to the enduring power of partnership. This was the bedrock of my understanding of family, the blueprint I carried into my own life.

Like my grandparents and parents, I married young, at twenty-three, filled with the optimism and belief in forever that such a foundation instills. Our family grew with the arrival of three wonderful children. We built a life together, culminating in the purchase of a five-bedroom house when I was thirty-one – my own version of the white picket fence, a symbol of the secure future I envisioned. This was Act One of my story, a period of growth, family, and the quiet contentment of building a life.

Then, the landscape began to shift, subtly at first, before the ground beneath me seemed to give way entirely. Act Two was a period where, looking back, it feels as though all hell simply broke loose. A company closure led to the loss of my job, a significant blow that coincided with a noticeable change in the dynamics of my marriage. The security I had felt began to crumble, culminating in the loss of our family home. For a time, I found myself living with my father-in-law, navigating a world that felt increasingly unfamiliar. In an attempt to reinvent myself, I even pursued a passion for cooking, studying to become a chef, but the financial realities of that path proved unsustainable. Eventually, I returned to the tech industry, a familiar landscape in a life that felt increasingly uncertain. Yet, the foundation of my marriage continued to erode, communication dwindling until it became sparse, if not entirely absent. The inevitable arrived when I made the difficult decision to leave and move out, followed by the formal filing for divorce. In an attempt to manage the financial strain, I initially sought the help of a paralegal, but this was misconstrued, leading to further complications. The ensuing legal proceedings were fraught with challenges, and I found myself financially devastated, a consequence of being the primary earner. For five years, I lived in a small, two-hundred-square-foot bedroom, a physical manifestation of the contraction in my life as I tried to cope with the seismic shift of divorce. Perhaps the most devastating aspect of this period was the time I missed with my children as they grew, a sacrifice that continues to resonate deeply. I felt a profound loss of purpose, a sense of being adrift in a sea of uncertainty.

Now, I find myself in Act Three, where the storm has largely passed, leaving behind a landscape that, while different, holds its own unexpected beauty. For over twelve years, I've carried the intention of writing this book, a period during which I've tried to absorb and note everything I encountered during and after my divorce – both the difficult and the surprisingly good. The result of that long process is this book, a journey through the complexities of divorce that, for me, was as much therapy as anything else. My aim in sharing my experiences and the insights I've gained is to shed light on the fact that divorce, while it can feel like the end, is often a turning point, a path that leads to unexpected and sometimes wonderful places.

Throughout these pages, you'll find no attempt to lay blame or point fingers. I've come to accept my own shortcomings in marriage and recognize that relationships are complex tapestries woven by two imperfect people. I should note that I am not a doctor or therapist, I'm simply sharing personal experiences and what I've learned and applied during this devastating process, offering tips and a recovery path of sorts that helped me find my way.

Some of what I share may or may not work for you, everyone's journey through divorce is uniquely their own. You may not relate to all of my experiences, but it is my sincere hope that parts of this book will illuminate your own path forward. If nothing else, know this: I do believe there is finality to even the most enveloping darkness and, eventually, a light that bathes you in comfort and love when you least expect it.

Throughout it all, my love for my children has remained unwavering. Today, I am deeply grateful that my relationship with them is stronger than ever, and I thank them profusely for allowing me to remain a part of their lives. I also want to extend my heartfelt gratitude to my parents, my relatives, and my close friends, who have consistently supported me through this challenging period. And finally, I want to thank my best friend and current spouse, MKS, for breathing new life into my soul and for showing me that love can indeed find its way back.

If you are reading this, you are likely navigating your own turbulent waters. Please know that I see you, I understand the complexities of what you are going through, and I truly care about your journey. This book is written with the hope that my experiences, my stumbles, and my eventual finding of a new path can offer you a sense of understanding, a glimmer of hope, and the reassurance that even after the storm, the journey continues, often leading to unexpected and beautiful destinations.

Chapter 1:
Acknowledging the Pain

The Weight of the Unspoken

The first subtle crack in the foundation of our marriage appeared on what seemed like an utterly ordinary Thursday afternoon. I can still recall the precise way the beginning of spring light slanted through the kitchen window, illuminating the tiny dust motes dancing in the air as my wife stood at the counter, her hands diligently chopping vegetables. This was to be the meal of our last anniversary together, a fact neither of us consciously acknowledged at the time. The rhythmic thunk of the knife against the wooden cutting board filled the otherwise quiet kitchen as I approached her from behind, drawn as I had been for nearly fifteen years by the familiar, comforting citrus scent of her shampoo. When I gently pressed a kiss to her shoulder – a gesture of affection that had become a near-daily ritual – her body stiffened. It was a slight movement, almost imperceptible, a mere fraction of an inch. Yet, that tiny, involuntary flinch sent an unexpected shockwave through the carefully constructed normalcy of our shared life.

I can still feel the cold dread that pooled in the pit of my stomach at that moment, a visceral response that I immediately tried to suppress. I remember forcing a light chuckle, asking about the details of her day as I reached for a glass, my hands trembling slightly as I poured myself a glass of Sunny Delight. She answered without turning to face me, her voice carrying a bright, almost cheerful tone, yet it felt distant, like a radio signal fading in and out of reception. Over time, we became experts at this intricate dance, maintaining the outward appearance of connection while meticulously avoiding any genuine emotional contact.

The psychologist Dr Sue Johnson eloquently describes these moments as "attachment injuries" – those seemingly small yet profoundly damaging instances when our fundamental sense of connection and security within a relationship gets fractured. For us, it wasn't a single, dramatic betrayal that caused the initial damage but rather a slow, insidious erosion, a death by a thousand paper cuts:

- The way her laughter at my jokes gradually transformed from the genuine, full-bodied belly laughs that used to make her smile with amusement into polite, almost perfunctory chuckles. It was a subtle shift, but it was one that spoke volumes about the changing dynamic between us.
- How our once cherished bedtime routine, which involved sharing each other's day, slowly morphed into a silent ritual of scrolling through separate phones in the quiet darkness, each lost in our own digital worlds, the shared stories replaced by individual distractions.
- The gradual realization that weeks had passed without any physical intimacy, a span that stretched into months, the absence becoming a heavy, unspoken presence in our shared bed.

The cruelest aspect of this slow unraveling was how convincingly normal everything appeared to the outside world. We continued going to family parties (both mine and hers), effortlessly playing the roles of the perfect couple, finishing each other's sentences and exchanging seemingly fond glances across the dinner table. We still exchanged anniversary cards, filled with loving messages written in careful, practiced cursive. We still shared a quick kiss goodbye each morning before heading off to work. But the kisses grew increasingly mechanical – quick pecks on the forehead like going off to school, devoid of the warmth and connection they once held. The cards contained inside jokes and loving sentiments from years past rather than reflecting the current state of our relationship. And the laughter that filled our home during family gatherings had an increasingly hollow ring like wind chimes moving without the touch of a genuine breeze.

My body, it seemed, knew the truth long before my conscious mind was willing to admit it. I developed chronic insomnia, lying awake night after night, watching the relentless march of the digital clock through the silent hours while she slept peacefully beside me, her steady breathing a taunting reminder of the profound intimacy we had lost. The unspoken stress even began to manifest physically. My hair began falling out in alarming clumps – so much so that my longtime friends and relatives gently inquired if I was experiencing unusual pressure, their concern evident in their glances at the thinning strands that were becoming increasingly noticeable on my scalp. A mysterious, persistent back pain settled between my shoulder blades like a stubborn, unwelcome houseguest, resistant to massage, medication, or even the most dedicated stretching practices I learned from a past personal trainer. I also began to gain weight without any conscious realization, and pounds kept adding on as food seemed to be the only comfort I could access – my favorite childhood dishes, which had always been a source of joy, now felt like the only companion I had.

Research sadly confirms that this physical manifestation of emotional distress is a common experience where they have found that individuals in distressed marriages often exhibit:

- Forty percent higher levels of stress hormones, such as cortisol, circulate throughout their bodies, indicating a state of chronic stress.

- Weakened immune systems, comparable to those of cancer patients undergoing treatment, highlight the profound impact of emotional strain on physical health.
- An increased risk of cardiovascular disease, equivalent to the risk associated with smoking a pack of cigarettes a day, underscoring the serious physical consequences of marital distress.
- Telomere shortening, which accelerates cellular aging by nearly a decade, suggests that prolonged emotional stress can have a significant impact on the body's aging process.

Yet, every morning, I would paste on a forced smile and offer a cheerful "Everything's great!" to concerned coworkers when they inquired about my weekend. I became an expert at deflection, skillfully changing the subject whenever friends grew too nosy, artfully pretending that our growing distance was just a temporary "rough patch" that all couples experience. But the lies we tell ourselves are often the most dangerous and insidious kind. "All marriages go through this," I'd silently reassure myself. "We're just busy with the kids." "It'll get better after this stressful period at work passes." Meanwhile, the gulf between us continued to widen until we were essentially living parallel lives within the same house – two strangers sharing a mailbox address and a collection of shared memories but little else of substance.

The night everything crystallized for me, the moment when the undeniable truth finally broke through the layers of denial wasn't marked by some dramatic confrontation or explosive argument. Instead, it was utterly mundane, which, in its own way, made it all the more devastating. We sat on opposite ends of our oversized sectional sofa, watching a romantic comedy on television. The three feet of empty cushion that stretched between us felt heavy with all the unspoken words, the unacknowledged distance. At one point, a particularly poignant scene unfolded on the screen – the kind of moment that, in years past, would have instinctively prompted us to reach for each other's hands, her fingers lacing through mine without a second thought. I glanced over at her and saw a single tear tracing a path down her cheek... while simultaneously, almost imperceptibly, she inched further away from me, seeking solace in the solitude of the armrest.

In that seemingly insignificant moment, I understood with a terrible, heartbreaking clarity: we weren't just slowly growing apart as ships passed in the night. We were actively, consciously retreating from each other, each seeking refuge in our own separate corners. The woman who once sought comfort on my shoulder now instinctively turned towards solitude. The man who used to memorize her intricate food preferences couldn't recall the last time they had engaged in a real, meaningful conversation about anything beyond the basic logistics of running a household.

What makes this stage of a failing marriage so agonizing is the pervasive cognitive dissonance. Part of you knows, deep down, exactly what is happening, while another part clings desperately to denial, desperately trying to maintain the illusion of normalcy. You become a master of:

- Selective memory: Focusing only on the happy moments from years past, those cherished memories that reinforce the narrative of a loving relationship, while consciously or unconsciously ignoring the present distance and the growing signs of disconnect.

- Downplaying concerns: Minimizing the significance of the growing distance and lack of connection, reassuring yourself that "all couples fight" as you sit through yet another silent meal, the unspoken tension hanging heavy in the air.
- Future-faking: Clinging to the hope that things will magically improve in the future, telling yourself that "things will be better when the kids are older," or "when we finally take that long-awaited vacation," or "when this stressful period at work finally passes," all the while ignoring the underlying issues that continue to fester.

The morning, I finally spoke the words aloud in the original draft doesn't quite capture the stark reality of how everything truly ended. The truth is, I had come home to yet another evening filled with a deafening silence, a silence that had become the unwelcome soundtrack to our lives. I finally mustered the courage to confront her, the question tumbling out, raw and desperate: "What's going on? Why won't you talk to me anymore?" It was as if that simple question finally broke the dam, and the floodgates of unspoken feelings burst open.

The conversation that followed was filled with tears from both of us, culminating in her devastating proclamation, "You tricked me into marrying you, and frankly, I don't love you. I don't know if I ever did." Those words tore through my heart, a pain more profound than any I had ever imagined. Moments after the weight of her confession settled upon me, our two youngest children, happy and playful as they often were, came into the bedroom, their smiles quickly fading as they took in the sight of both their mom and dad with tears streaming down their faces. "What's wrong, Dad?" my youngest asked, their small voice filled with concern. My daughter, her smile vanishing, turned towards her mother in total confusion, simply uttering, "Mom?" Those words of my wife's echoed relentlessly in my mind, leaving me in a state of utter shock and disbelief. My heart sank with the crushing weight of her admission. Everything we had built together over nineteen years of marriage, the countless memories we had created, the love I believed we shared now felt like nothing more than a distant and fragile dream, shattered into a million irreparable pieces in a single, agonizing moment.

Looking back, I can trace the slow, almost imperceptible unraveling of our connection through the disappearing "we" in our conversations about building our life and our shared ventures:

- Year 1: "We should absolutely invest in this new business opportunity together! Imagine the future we can build for our family!"
- Year 5: "I think it would be smart for *us* to consider diversifying our investments; maybe you can focus on your career growth while I explore this side venture."
- Year 10: "You should really consider that new role – it aligns perfectly with your skills. I've been thinking about restructuring my business in a way that gives me more flexibility."

Grief experts often talk about "anticipatory mourning" – the quiet, often subconscious process of grieving something before it is actually gone. That's what those final months, and perhaps even years, felt like. I wasn't just slowly losing my wife; I was also losing the future we had planned together – the cozy retirement home, the leisurely European trip we'd promised ourselves for our twenty-fifth anniversary, the very family identity we had built, the "team us" that used to tackle life's challenges side-by-side. I was even losing the version of myself that existed only in relation to her, the man who knew exactly how to make her laugh until her stomach hurt, the one who felt complete in her presence.

The weight of all those unspoken goodbyes, those silent acknowledgments of our diverging paths, nearly crushed me. The last time we made love (had I known it was the last, would I have held her gaze just a moment longer, memorized the feel of her hand in mine?). The last time she called me "hon" with that particular lilt in her voice, a term of endearment that had once felt so uniquely ours. I hadn't known to mark those moments as endings, so they simply slipped away, unnoticed, until their absence became a palpable presence all its own, a void that echoed with what was no longer.

Now, when I look back at photos from that final year of our marriage, what strikes me most isn't the smiles we outwardly projected for the camera – it's the ever-increasing space between our bodies in every picture. The subtle, almost unconscious way we positioned ourselves just slightly out of reach in family portraits. How our hands rarely touched anymore, even when we were posing with the kids, trying to maintain the illusion of a happy family. Two people standing together, side-by-side, yet already profoundly alone, smiling for the camera while our eyes, if you looked closely enough, told a completely different story.

The psychologist Robert Weiss poignantly describes this state as "living in the shadow of the past and the ghost of the future." (https://pmc.ncbi.nlm.nih.gov/articles/PMC3459997/) We weren't truly present with each other anymore, not in any meaningful way – just going through the motions, performing the familiar rituals of coupledom while silently grieving what had been and simultaneously dreading the inevitable arrival of what was to come. The weight of all that unspoken sorrow, that underlying fear and the quiet ache of regret was heavier than any single dramatic fight or heated argument could ever be.

The Ripple Effects No One Mentions: Extended Family and Social Fallout

While we braced ourselves for the inevitable pain our children would experience, the fallout within our extended family unfolded in ways I hadn't fully anticipated. I had always maintained an excellent relationship with my father-in-law. His own wife, my ex-wife's mother, had been absent from their lives since my ex and her sister were toddlers, so my connection with my father-in-law had always been strong. I was especially grateful to him for allowing us to live in his home after we lost our own. In the immediate aftermath of our devastating confrontation, I went straight to his room to let him know that I could no longer cope with his daughter and that the months of silence culminating in her confession had driven me to leave. Even he was tearful about the situation, expressing his sadness over how things had deteriorated. You have to understand our issues were never rooted in anger or infidelity. I never yelled, never resorted to name-calling, and was always faithful. The core of our struggles, in the end, seemed to revolve around financial matters; I'm sure there were other factors as well.

As for my brother and sister-in-laws, my departure was abrupt and without explanation. I simply disappeared from their lives. To this day, I have no idea what, if anything, was said or explained to them about my absence or the reason for our divorce. My own parents were, of course, deeply saddened by the news. They had both grown to love my ex-wife very much, and the end of our marriage was a source of considerable heartache for them as well.

Our social life wasn't really a shared entity. I had my own close circle of friends, and my ex-wife had hers, many of whom were her clients. However, I did make sure to personally inform her cousin, who had been my best man at our wedding and remains one of my dearest and closest friends to this day, about the difficult turn our lives had taken.

The Unexpected Silver Linings: From Ashes, Superpowers Emerge

The aftermath of divorce, while undoubtedly a period of profound loss and significant upheaval, also unexpectedly became a crucible for intense personal growth and surprising discovery. It was a time when the familiar structures of our lives crumbled, forcing each of us to confront our individual selves and, ultimately, to rebuild our lives from the ground up. In this challenging process, my children, with an almost uncanny resilience, developed remarkable levels of emotional intelligence, qualities that I now fondly refer to as their "post-traumatic superpowers."

My eldest son, my firstborn, initially became somewhat withdrawn, retreating into his own thoughts during moments of conflict. However, with time and his own inner strength, he gradually blossomed into a surprisingly open and socially adept young man. He learned, with a maturity that belied his young age, to navigate the complexities of his peer relationships, often acting as a natural mediator in disputes, demonstrating a remarkable ability to find common ground and facilitate peaceful resolutions. He seemed to instinctively understand the delicate balance of compromise, the subtle nuances of human interaction, skills that were undoubtedly honed through navigating the ever-shifting and sometimes turbulent landscape of our fractured family. He would often articulate this newfound wisdom with a simple yet profound philosophy: "If we can each give a little, everyone wins a little," a statement that spoke volumes about his evolving understanding of human dynamics and his innate ability to build bridges where others might only see divides.

My daughter, my second child, had always possessed a quiet strength, a resilience I recognized as a beautiful echo of her mother's own inner fortitude. Through the challenges of our divorce, this inherent resilience shone even brighter. She developed a truly remarkable capacity for emotional nuance. Even at a young age, she could articulate the subtle yet significant differences between feeling "lonely" and simply being "just alone," a level of self-awareness and emotional literacy that many adults continue to struggle to achieve. She learned, through careful observation and quiet introspection, to differentiate between the aching desire for connection and the peaceful solitude of quiet contemplation. This artistic soul also blossomed into an amazing artist, a passion that eventually led her to graduate summa cum laude from her class at the university, a testament to her dedication and talent.

My youngest son, always a jolly and naturally social child, also developed his own unique "superpower" during this time: a striking degree of radical honesty and a remarkable refusal to tolerate even the slightest hint of insincerity in his interactions with the world around him. He became surprisingly adept at spotting what he termed "fake nice",particularly from the parents of his divorced friends, who often seemed to try a little too hard to project an image of perfect harmony and effortless co-parenting. He would often exchange knowing glances, a silent language passing between them, and whisper with a wisdom beyond his years, "They're trying way too hard." This wasn't simply an act of childhood cynicism; it was a powerful testament to his developing ability to see through superficial facades, to value genuine connection, even when it was messy or imperfect, above the often-unrealistic expectations of forced pleasantries.

All three of my children, in their own individual ways, emerged from the difficulties of our divorce with remarkable emotional intelligence and an inner strength that continues to fill me with immense pride. They truly are my unexpected silver linings.

My Own Phoenix Moments: Rebirth in the Embers

My personal journey of healing and self-discovery in the aftermath of our divorce was, in its own way, equally transformative, a slow and often arduous process of rediscovering myself amidst what felt like the complete wreckage of my former life. The quiet desperation of countless 3 AM insomnia sessions, those long, dark hours when sleep seemed an impossible luxury, unexpectedly became an unlikely catalyst for creative expression. I found myself drawn back to my long-neglected love for the guitar, slowly relearning intricate fingerpicking patterns that had lain dormant for years, buried beneath the weight of responsibility and unspoken sorrow. The soothing melodies that filled the quiet rental became a form of unexpected meditation, a tangible and beautiful way to channel the restless energy of grief and the persistent ache of loneliness into something that felt both meaningful and deeply personal. This wasn't simply a way to pass the time; it was a profound reclamation of a lost part of myself, a quiet reconnection with the creative spirit that had always resided within me.

My stoic neighbor, a man of few words who had always maintained a polite but somewhat distant presence, surprised me one Saturday morning with an unexpected act of quiet kindness. He simply showed up at my doorstep, tools in hand, offering his silent assistance in assembling a particularly complex piece of flat-pack Ikea furniture, a task that had been looming over me like a metaphor for the overwhelming feeling of having to rebuild everything from scratch. His quiet, unassuming presence and his willingness to share the physical burden without offering any unsolicited advice or well-meaning platitudes became an unexpected lifeline during a time when I felt profoundly alone. This wasn't just a neighborly gesture; it was a profound act of human solidarity, a silent acknowledgment of the unspoken struggle I was facing.

At work, I found myself channeling the raw and often overwhelming emotions of my divorce into a newfound and intense focus on the tasks at hand. If anything, meticulous attention to detail became my unexpected anchor in the storm. Where I might have previously approached projects with a broader stroke, I now found myself immersed in the minutiae, double-checking every aspect, meticulously planning each step, and ensuring nothing was overlooked. My boss, who has been more of a friend than a supervisor for decades, truly became an unwavering pillar of support during this incredibly challenging period. He understood the immense pressure I was under, not just professionally but personally, and his incredibly generous offer of a room at his then-condo when I first moved out from my father-in-law's house was a lifeline, a tangible act of friendship that, while I didn't ultimately take him up on it, provided an immense amount of comfort and reassurance during a time when my own world felt like it was constantly shifting. I became more driven than ever before to not only ensure the successful completion of projects but to execute them with an exceptional level of thoroughness and responsibility. Managing resources with precision and adhering strictly to budgets became top priorities, not just as professional obligations but as a way to exert control and find a sense of accomplishment in a world that often felt chaotic. This wasn't about aggressively pursuing promotions or climbing the corporate ladder but rather about finding solid ground and a sense of purpose in my professional life amidst the personal upheaval, a place where I could feel a sense of control and achieve tangible results.

Closing: The First Step Toward Healing, Naming the Pain

Healing, I've come to understand, truly begins with the often-difficult act of acknowledging the pain, giving it a name and allowing it to have a voice. A compelling study conducted at Stanford University revealed that participants who consciously journaled about their divorce for just fifteen minutes each day experienced a remarkably thirty percent faster recovery, as measured by their cortisol levels, compared to those who actively suppressed their emotions and tried to pretend everything was alright. This wasn't just an interesting statistic; it was a powerful and scientifically backed affirmation of the profound importance of actively processing grief and allowing ourselves to feel the full weight of our experiences. Your pain, whatever form it takes, needs to be witnessed, not silenced or ignored; it needs to be acknowledged, explored with honesty, and ultimately, understood with compassion.

Your Grounding Assignment: A Path to Self-Discovery

To help you begin this crucial process of acknowledging your own pain and starting your journey towards healing, I encourage you to engage with the following grounding exercises:

- **Body Scan:** Take a quiet moment to gently scan your body, paying close attention to any physical sensations that might be holding onto the residue of your grief. Is there a persistent knot of tension in your jaw, a noticeable tightness in your chest, or a dull, persistent ache in your stomach? Simply pay attention to these physical manifestations of your emotions, acknowledging their presence without judgment or the need to immediately fix them. This isn't just a simple exercise; it's a way to reconnect with your body's innate wisdom to understand the profound ways in which your emotions are often physically expressed.

- **"Before & After" List:** Take some time to create a list that thoughtfully compares your beliefs and expectations about love and marriage before your divorce with your current understanding of relationships, shaped by your recent experiences. Reflect honestly on the illusions that may have been shattered, the brutal truths you have learned about yourself and others, and the new perspectives you have gained about connection and commitment. This isn't just a superficial reflection; it's a crucial process of redefining your understanding of love, relationships, and your own needs within them, creating a new and more realistic framework for future connections.

- **One Permission Slip:** Write yourself a permission slip, granting yourself the unconditional permission to feel, to heal at your own pace, and to simply be human in all your messy complexity. Perhaps it reads: "I hereby grant myself permission to grieve the loss of my marriage for as long as I need." Or maybe: "I am absolutely allowed to feel angry, sad, confused, or even a little lost right now." Or perhaps simply: "I give myself permission to prioritize my own well-being, without guilt or apology." This isn't just an act of self-indulgence; it's a profound act of self-compassion, a gentle recognition of your own inherent humanity and your right to navigate this challenging time with grace and understanding.

Final Truth: Embracing the Messy Reality

True healing, I believe, begins when you consciously stop comparing your own deeply personal internal reality to the often carefully curated and highly selective external images of others. That seemingly Instagram-perfect blended family you might see online? They undoubtedly have their own 3 AM terrors, their own hidden struggles and unspoken anxieties. The ex-partner who appears to be completely unfazed by the divorce? They are either navigating their own pain in a different way, perhaps even masking their true feelings beneath a carefully constructed facade of composure. Your pain, in all its messy and sometimes overwhelming reality, isn't a sign of weakness or failure; rather, it is a powerful testament to your profound capacity for love and your incredible courage to bravely face significant loss. It is, in its own way, the undeniable proof that you possess the remarkable ability to feel deeply, to heal authentically, and ultimately, to grow into an even stronger and more compassionate version of yourself. It is proof that you are, at your core, deeply human, undeniably strong, and absolutely capable of building a beautiful and fulfilling future from the fragments of the past.

A Message of Hope: The Voice Within

Because here's what I desperately wish someone had told me in those darkest moments of my own journey, what I so profoundly needed to hear when the weight of it all felt utterly unbearable: The simple fact that you are still breathing through this pain, that you are putting one foot in front of the other each day, means that you are far stronger than you currently believe. The fact that you worry about the well-being of your children or others who may be affected and that you are grappling with how to best support them through this challenging time means that you are already breaking negative cycles and actively building a new foundation of love and care for them. The fact that you are reading these very words right now means that a part of you, however small, still believes in the possibility of healing, that a tiny flicker of hope remains alive amidst the ashes of your former life.

And that part of you? That persistent flicker of hope, that quiet but unwavering voice that whispers within your heart, is the one to listen to now, more than any other. It is the voice of your inherent resilience, the voice of your undeniable strength, the voice of your enduring capacity for love and for profound healing. It is the voice that will gently guide you through the darkness that will ultimately lead you toward the light of a new and hopeful beginning. It is the voice that softly whispers, "You are not alone in this. You are not irreparably broken. You are absolutely capable of rebuilding your life, of finding joy again, and of creating a future that is uniquely and beautifully yours." Listen intently to that voice. Trust that voice. It is your compass, your most reliable guide, your unwavering lifeline in the days and weeks ahead.

Closing: The First Step Toward Healing, A Foundation Built on Truth

This chapter wasn't about offering quick fixes or neatly packaged solutions to the complex pain of divorce. It wasn't about pretending that healing is a linear and predictable journey with clearly defined milestones. Instead, it was, and remains, about truth, raw, unfiltered, and sometimes agonizingly painful. Before we can even begin to consider the possibility of rebuilding our lives and moving forward with intention, we must first acknowledge the full and often devastating extent of the emotional wreckage. We must allow ourselves to truly see the shattered fragments of our once-cherished expectations, to fully feel the crushing weight of the grief that often threatens to engulf us entirely, and to recognize the innocent children who are often caught in the painful crossfire of our unraveling lives. To deny these harsh realities, to try to bypass the necessary process of acknowledging our pain, is ultimately to deny ourselves the genuine opportunity for true and lasting healing.

The process of acknowledging this devastation, of truly facing the depth of our pain, is not a passive act; it requires a conscious, deliberate, and often courageous effort. It demands that we confront the uncomfortable truths we have likely been desperately trying to avoid, to gently peel back the protective layers of denial and self-deception that have served as temporary shields against the raw intensity of our emotions. It means finally admitting, perhaps only to ourselves in the quiet of our own thoughts, that we are not "fine," that we are not just "coping" as we might outwardly project, and that we are, in fact, deeply wounded by the experiences we have endured.

This honest acknowledgment of our pain is not a sign of weakness or failure; rather, it is a profound testament to our inherent courage, our unwavering resilience, and our deep capacity for authentic self-awareness. It is, in its own way, the very first and most crucial step on the long and often challenging path toward reclaiming our lives, toward building a future that is not forever defined by the wreckage of the past but rather illuminated by the lessons learned and the strength we have discovered within ourselves.

Reflection Questions: A Path to Self-Understanding

This chapter has explored the fundamental importance of acknowledging the often-overwhelming pain of divorce as the very first step towards healing, as well as a glimpse of my own personal journey. To help you connect with your own unique experience and begin this crucial process of honest acknowledgment and compassionate self-inquiry, I encourage you to consider the following reflection questions. Remember, there are no right or wrong answers here. This is a safe and private space for you to explore your inner landscape without judgment.

- **What is the most prominent emotion you've been experiencing since the divorce?** Divorce can trigger a whirlwind of emotions, often shifting and swirling like a storm. Take a moment to identify the feeling that has been most dominant for you since your separation. Is it a deep sadness that feels like a constant weight? Perhaps a burning anger that flares up unexpectedly? Or maybe a sense of fear and uncertainty about the future? It could also be confusion, a feeling of being lost and unsure of what comes next, or even a sense of relief, especially if the marriage was deeply unhappy. Naming this prominent emotion is the first step towards understanding its impact on you and beginning the process of acknowledging and processing it. Allow yourself to recognize this feeling without judgment or the need to change it immediately. *Aha moment: Simply naming the most prominent emotion can bring a sense of clarity and validation to your experience.*

- **What is one thing you've been avoiding feeling?** It's a natural human tendency to try and shield ourselves from emotions that feel too overwhelming or painful. However, avoidance, while offering temporary relief, can often prolong the healing process in the long run. Gently consider if there is a particular emotion, or set of emotions, that you've been consciously or unconsciously pushing away since your divorce. Perhaps it's the raw grief of losing a shared future you had envisioned, the deep-seated fear of being alone and navigating life independently, or the intense anger at your former partner or even yourself for what has transpired. Acknowledging this avoided emotion, even if it feels uncomfortable to bring it to the surface, can be a crucial step in allowing yourself to fully heal. *Aha moment: Recognizing the emotion you've been avoiding can unlock a deeper understanding of your underlying pain.*

- **Where in your body do you feel the pain of the divorce?** Our emotions are not just abstract feelings; they often manifest in very real physical sensations within our bodies. Take a moment to tune into your physical self. Where do you notice any tension, discomfort, or pain? Do you feel a persistent tightness in your chest, a heavy knot in your stomach, a constant tension in your shoulders, or perhaps a dull ache in your head? Connecting with these physical sensations can provide valuable insights into the emotional pain you are carrying. Your body often holds onto emotions that your mind might try to suppress, so paying attention to these signals can be a powerful way to ground yourself in your present emotional state and bring awareness to the areas where you might need to offer yourself extra care and attention. *Aha moment: Noticing the physical manifestations of your emotional pain can create a deeper connection to your feelings.*

- **What is one loss you are grieving that might not be obvious to others?** Divorce involves a multitude of losses, many of which extend beyond the obvious ending of the marital relationship itself. Think about some of the less tangible losses you might be experiencing, losses that might not be immediately apparent to those around you. Perhaps it's the loss of a sense of security and stability, the loss of shared dreams and future plans you had envisioned together, the loss of a certain identity you held within the marriage, or the loss of a familiar routine and daily companionship. Identifying these less visible losses can help you validate the full scope of your grief and acknowledge the depth of what you are navigating. Giving voice to these hidden losses, even if only to yourself, can be a significant step in honoring your complete experience. *Aha moment:* *Identifying a less obvious loss can validate the depth and complexity of your grief.*

- **What is one small act of self-compassion you can offer yourself right now?** In the midst of navigating the often-turbulent waters of divorce, practicing self-compassion is absolutely crucial. Think about one small, tangible act of kindness and care that you can offer yourself at this very moment. It doesn't need to be grand or time-consuming. Perhaps it's taking a few deep, calming breaths, wrapping yourself in a cozy blanket, allowing yourself a few moments of quiet rest, reaching out to a supportive friend, or simply offering yourself some gentle, encouraging words. This small act of self-compassion can provide a much-needed moment of comfort and remind you that you deserve kindness and understanding, especially during this challenging time. *Aha moment: Recognizing that even a small act of self-compassion can provide immediate comfort and support.*

Chapter 2:

Navigating Through the Storm

The Silent Tempest

Divorce marks the end of a partnership, a significant life chapter closing. However, it also signifies the unraveling of shared dreams, the dissolution of a future once envisioned, and the loss of a carefully constructed life framework. The pain that follows is profound, deeply personal, and often isolating. You may find yourself standing amidst the remnants of a life that no longer feels familiar, questioning how to navigate the uncharted territory ahead.

It's crucial to understand this: your pain is valid. It is a natural and understandable response to a significant loss.

In contemporary culture, there's often an unspoken expectation to "move on" swiftly, as if grief were a sign of weakness or an inconvenience to be quickly discarded. However, healing doesn't adhere to such rigid timelines or societal pressures. One cannot rush through emotions or pretend they don't exist. True healing necessitates confronting the pain, allowing oneself to feel the full spectrum of emotions: the anger, the sorrow, and even the unsettling numbness.

This chapter is about granting yourself permission to acknowledge the hurt without judgment. It's about creating a safe space for your emotions and recognizing that before healing can truly commence, the pain must first be recognized, validated, and understood.

Understanding the Layers of Divorce Grief: A Complex Tapestry

Divorce grief is not a singular, monolithic emotion. Instead, it manifests as a complex tapestry, interwoven with various threads of loss that contribute to a profound sense of disorientation. It's essential to recognize that this grief extends far beyond the dissolution of a romantic partnership. It encompasses the dismantling of an entire life structure, a carefully constructed system of routines, expectations, and deeply ingrained shared dreams.

Unlike the grief that follows a death, divorce grief often lacks the societal acknowledgment and rituals that provide a framework for mourning. This absence of formal mourning can lead to a sense of isolation, where individuals feel their pain is unseen and invalidated. Well-meaning individuals may minimize the experience, failing to grasp the depth of the emotional upheaval. This societal lack of understanding can intensify the grieving process, leaving individuals to navigate their pain in silence.

The complexity of divorce grief stems from the multitude of losses it entails. Furthermore, divorce grief is often compounded by the ongoing presence of the former partner. Unlike death, where closure is more definitive, divorce leaves the grieving individual to navigate a world where the source of their pain remains. This can lead to persistent reminders, triggering emotional responses and hindering the healing process.

It is vital to approach divorce grief with a compassionate understanding of its intricate nature. Recognizing the multitude of layers involved allows for a more comprehensive approach to healing. It emphasizes the need for self-compassion, patience, and a willingness to acknowledge the validity of the emotional experience.

The Five Major Losses in Divorce: A Framework for Understanding

To better understand the intricate nature of divorce grief, it's helpful to recognize the five major categories of losses that often accompany this experience:

- **Loss of Identity:** Who are you now, independent of this relationship? How do you redefine yourself when a role you once held, a label you once wore, no longer exists? This loss can create a profound sense of disorientation and uncertainty.
- **Loss of Daily Routine:** The absence of shared rituals, the morning coffee, the evening conversations, the comforting routines that structured your days. The silence where there was once companionship, the emptiness where there was once shared activity.
- **Loss of Shared Dreams:** The plans for the future that will now go unfulfilled, the shared aspirations that have been irrevocably altered. The sense of security that came with believing in "forever," the foundation of which has been shaken.
- **Loss of Social Connections:** The friends who distance themselves, unsure of how to navigate the shifting dynamics, or those who take sides, creating further divisions. The shifting relationships with

extended family, the awkward encounters, and the sense of isolation.

- **Loss of Trust:** The shattered trust in your former partner, the questioning of your own judgment, and the erosion of belief in the possibility of lasting love. This loss can create a sense of vulnerability and fear, making it difficult to open oneself to future relationships.

Why Divorce Grief Feels Different: The Absence of Ritual

The experience of grief following a divorce is distinct from other forms of loss, largely due to the absence of established societal rituals that typically accompany mourning. In the case of death, for example, there are funerals, wakes, and memorial services that provide a structured framework for grieving. These rituals offer a communal space for acknowledging loss, expressing sorrow, and beginning the process of acceptance. However, divorce lacks such formal rites of passage, leaving individuals to navigate their grief in a social vacuum.

This absence of ritual can create a sense of disorientation and isolation. Without clear societal guidelines, individuals may struggle to understand the legitimacy of their grief, questioning whether their pain is valid. They may feel pressured to "move on" quickly as if their emotional response is inappropriate or excessive. This lack of validation can compound the already complex emotions associated with divorce, leading to feelings of disenfranchisement and misunderstanding.

Furthermore, the person being grieved in a divorce is often still present in the world, leading to a unique form of prolonged ambiguity. Unlike death, where the finality of loss is more defined, divorce involves navigating a world where the former partner continues to exist. This can trigger ongoing emotional responses, making closure a more elusive and complicated process. Shared spaces, mutual friends, and even social media can serve as constant reminders of the lost relationship, hindering the ability to fully process grief.

The absence of ritual also impacts the way society perceives and responds to divorce grief. There is often a tendency to minimize the experience, urging individuals to "just get over it" or to focus on the "positive" aspects of being single again. This lack of understanding can further isolate those who are grieving, making it difficult for them to find the support and validation they need. Without clear societal markers of mourning, the grieving process following a divorce becomes a deeply personal and often solitary journey.

The Weight of Unspoken Grief: The Burden of Misunderstanding

Divorce grief often becomes an invisible burden, a silent suffering carried by individuals who find their pain minimized or dismissed by those around them. Unlike the more recognized grief associated with death, divorce grief frequently lacks societal validation. This lack of acknowledgment can amplify emotional turmoil, creating a sense of isolation and misunderstanding. Well-intentioned individuals, often unaware of the depth of the loss, may offer platitudes that inadvertently invalidate the grieving process.

Phrases like "You'll find someone better," "At least you're free now," or "Everything happens for a reason," while meant to be comforting, often serve to minimize the profound emotional upheaval experienced during divorce. These statements fail to recognize the intricate layers of loss involved, the loss of dreams, routines, and a sense of security, and instead encourage a rapid return to normalcy. This pressure to "move on" can create a sense of internal conflict, where individuals feel their grief is not only painful but also inappropriate.

The burden of unspoken grief is compounded by the lack of societal understanding of the unique challenges divorce presents. Unlike the clear-cut finality of death, divorce involves navigating a world where the former partner still exists, potentially leading to ongoing interactions and reminders of the lost relationship. This ambiguity can prolong the grieving process, making it difficult to achieve closure.

Furthermore, the societal tendency to frame divorce as a failure or a personal shortcoming adds another layer of emotional weight. Individuals may internalize these judgments, leading to feelings of shame and self-blame. They may hesitate to express their grief openly, fearing they will be perceived as weak or incapable of moving forward.

The result is silent suffering, where individuals feel compelled to suppress their emotions, leading to further isolation and hindering the healing process. This unspoken grief underscores the need for greater awareness and empathy in understanding the complexities of divorce, recognizing it as a significant loss that requires time, understanding, and compassionate support.

Exercise: Mapping Your Grief, A Journey of Self-Discovery

To begin the process of acknowledging and understanding your grief, consider taking time to reflect on your experience by answering the following questions:

- **Where do you feel grief in your body?** Is it a tightness in your chest, a heaviness in your limbs, a knot in your stomach? Pay attention to the physical manifestations of your emotional pain.
- **What emotions arise most often?** Anger, sadness, relief, guilt, confusion? Identify the dominant emotions that surface during this time.
- **What triggers unexpected waves of grief?** A song, a place, a date on the calendar, a scent? Recognize the triggers that evoke powerful emotional responses.
- **When have you felt moments of relief?** Who or what provided comfort during these moments? Identify the sources of solace and support.

This exercise isn't about solving anything; it's about honoring what you're feeling acknowledging the validity of your emotional experience.

Anger: The Fire That Burns and Purifies, A Necessary Emotion

Anger, often perceived as a destructive force, is frequently misunderstood in the context of healing, particularly following a divorce. Many are advised to "let it go," as if it were an emotion to be discarded or suppressed. However, anger serves a critical purpose in the grieving process. It is a potent signal, a visceral response that alerts us to injustice, hurt, and violated boundaries. To deny or suppress this emotion is to ignore a vital part of the healing journey.

The protective role of anger is paramount. It arises as a natural defense, signaling that you were wronged, that your trust was betrayed, or that your expectations were shattered. It is not the enemy but rather a messenger demanding attention and action. Anger, in its rawest form, illuminates the areas where you were hurt, prompting you to acknowledge the pain and begin the process of setting new boundaries.

The spectrum of anger experienced during divorce is broad and varied. Righteous anger may surface in response to betrayal or unfair treatment, a burning sense of injustice that demands recognition. Protest anger arises from a deep-seated need to make your pain visible, to have it acknowledged and validated. Self-directed anger, often expressed as "Why didn't I see this coming?" reflects internal questioning and self-blame. Existential anger, a rage at the unfairness of the situation, challenges the very foundations of your understanding of the world.

Processing anger constructively is essential. Physical release through exercise or other activities can help channel the intense energy. Creative expression, such as writing, painting, or music, provides an outlet for transforming the emotion into something tangible. Constructive action, using anger to set new boundaries or fuel personal growth, allows you to reclaim agency and control.

Anger, when understood and processed healthily, is not something to be feared. It is a powerful catalyst for change, a sign that your spirit is fighting for its worth, demanding to be heard. It is a necessary fire that burns away the remnants of the past, paving the way for healing and renewal.

The Protective Role of Anger: A Signal of Injustice

Anger, in the context of divorce, often arises as a natural protective mechanism, acting as a powerful signal that boundaries have been violated and injustices have occurred. It's a visceral response, a surge of energy that demands attention, highlighting areas where one has been wronged or deeply hurt. This emotion, rather than being inherently destructive, serves to illuminate the need for self-preservation and the establishment of new, healthier boundaries.

When trust is broken, when promises are shattered, or when fundamental expectations are disregarded, anger emerges as a clear indicator that something is amiss. It's a call to action, urging individuals to recognize the pain inflicted upon them and to acknowledge the violation of their personal space. This recognition is crucial for healing, as it validates the emotional experience and prevents the internalization of blame.

Anger, in this context, is not a sign of weakness or a failure to cope. It's a healthy and appropriate response to perceived injustice. It signals that one's sense of fairness has been compromised and that one's emotional well-being has been disregarded. It acts as a defense mechanism, preventing further emotional erosion and empowering individuals to assert their needs.

This emotion also serves as a catalyst for change. It prompts individuals to reevaluate their relationships, identify patterns of behavior that are detrimental to their well-being, and establish new guidelines for future interactions. By acknowledging and processing anger, individuals can reclaim their sense of agency and begin the process of rebuilding their lives on a foundation of self-respect and self-preservation.

In essence, anger acts as a potent signal, alerting individuals to the injustices they have experienced during divorce.

It is not an emotion to be feared or suppressed but rather a powerful tool for self-protection and a necessary step on the path to healing.

Types of Anger in Divorce: A Spectrum of Emotion

- **Righteous Anger:** Fury over betrayal, unfair treatment, or injustice.
- **Protest Anger:** The desperate need to make your pain visible, to have it acknowledged.
- **Self-Directed Anger:** "Why didn't I see this coming?" The internal questioning and self-blame.
- **Existential Anger:** Rage at the unfairness of the situation, the sense of meaninglessness.

Healthy Ways to Process Anger: Transforming Energy

- **Physical Release:** Exercise, screaming into a pillow, hitting a punching bag, channeling the energy into physical activity.
- **Creative Expression:** Writing, painting, music, transforming the emotion into art.
- **Constructive Action:** Using the anger to set new boundaries, fuel personal growth, and advocate for oneself.

Anger isn't something to fear; it's a sign that your spirit is fighting for its worth, demanding to be heard.

The Hollow Days: When Numbness Takes Over, A Protective Mechanism

In the wake of divorce, the emotional landscape can become overwhelming, a tempest of conflicting feelings that threaten to engulf the individual. Amidst the surges of anger, sadness, and fear, there often emerge periods of profound numbness, the "hollow days" when emotions seem to vanish, leaving behind an unsettling emptiness. This numbness, far from being a sign of emotional detachment or failure, is often a crucial protective mechanism, a temporary reprieve from the intensity of grief.

Numbness arises as a natural response when the emotional system becomes overloaded, a form of self-preservation that allows the mind to cope with an otherwise unbearable reality. It's akin to a circuit breaker, preventing a complete emotional meltdown by temporarily shutting down the flow of feeling. During these hollow days, life can take on a muted quality, as if viewed through a thick fog. The activities that once brought joy seem devoid of meaning, and the world itself can feel distant and unreal.

This emotional detachment is not a conscious choice but rather an involuntary response to extreme stress. The mind, in its wisdom, recognizes the need for a pause, a moment of stillness amidst the chaos. It's a way of saying, "I cannot process any more right now." This pause allows the individual to conserve energy to avoid being completely consumed by the intensity of their emotions.

It's important to recognize that numbness is not a sign of weakness or apathy. It's a temporary state, a necessary part of the grieving process. However, it's also essential to be mindful of its duration. Prolonged numbness, lasting for weeks without relief, can indicate a need for professional support. Similarly, if numbness leads to harmful behaviors as a means of seeking any sensation, it's crucial to seek help.

Navigating the hollow days requires patience and self-compassion. Small acts of reconnection, such as focusing on sensory experiences like the warmth of a bath or the taste of a favorite food, can help to gently reawaken the senses. Compassionate observation, acknowledging the numbness without judgment, can also provide a sense of acceptance.

Ultimately, the hollow days are a temporary phase, a necessary pause before the journey of healing continues. They are a testament to the mind's resilience and its ability to protect itself in the face of overwhelming emotional stress.

Why Numbness Happens: A Mind's Shield

Numbness, during the tumultuous period following a divorce, is not a mere absence of feeling; it's a complex, multifaceted response orchestrated by the mind as a protective shield against overwhelming emotional pain. When faced with the intense, often conflicting emotions that accompany divorce, the brain can activate a kind of "circuit breaker," temporarily disconnecting from the full spectrum of feeling to prevent a catastrophic overload.

This mechanism is deeply rooted in our evolutionary biology. When confronted with extreme stress, the brain prioritizes survival. In the context of divorce, where the very foundations of one's life may feel shattered, the mind perceives a threat to emotional stability. Numbness acts as a form of emotional anesthesia, dulling the sharp edges of pain and allowing the individual to function, at least on a basic level, during a period of intense vulnerability.

Psychologically, numbness can be understood as a form of dissociation. When emotions become too intense to process, the mind creates a sense of detachment from those feelings, as if observing them from a distance. This dissociation serves to create a buffer, a space between the individual and the overwhelming emotional reality. It's a way of saying, "I cannot handle this right now," and creating a temporary emotional "off" switch.

The brain's stress response system, involving the hypothalamic-pituitary-adrenal (HPA) axis, plays a crucial role in this process. When faced with prolonged or intense stress, the HPA axis releases cortisol and other stress hormones. While these hormones are initially adaptive, helping us to respond to threats, chronic stress can lead to dysregulation of the HPA axis. This dysregulation can manifest as emotional numbness, as the brain attempts to dampen its response to overwhelming input.

Furthermore, numbness can be a form of learned helplessness. After experiencing repeated or prolonged emotional pain, the mind may conclude that feeling is futile, leading to a kind of emotional shutdown. This learned helplessness can contribute to a sense of apathy and detachment, further perpetuating the cycle of numbness.

It is crucial to recognize that numbness is not a sign of weakness or failure. It's a natural, albeit sometimes problematic, response to extreme emotional distress. However, prolonged numbness can hinder the healing process, preventing the necessary processing of emotions. Understanding the neurological and psychological underpinnings of numbness can help individuals approach this state with compassion and seek appropriate support when needed.

Signs You're in the Hollow Days: Emotional Detachment

- Life feels muted as if you're observing from a distance.
- Things that once brought joy now feel meaningless, devoid of pleasure.
- You go through the motions without feeling present, without genuine engagement.

Navigating Numbness: Reconnecting with Self

- **Small Acts of Reconnection:** Focus on sensory experiences, the warmth of the water, the taste of food, and the feel of the fabric.
- **Compassionate Observation:** "I notice I'm feeling numb right now. That's okay." Acknowledge the state without judgment.
- **When to Seek Support:** If numbness persists for weeks without relief or if you're engaging in harmful behaviors to feel something.

Remember, the hollow days won't last forever. They are a temporary part of the process, a necessary pause before the journey continues.

Guilt and Shame: The Silent Struggles, The Internal Critic

Beneath the overt expressions of grief, anger, sadness, and numbness often lurk the insidious whispers of guilt and shame. These silent struggles, stemming from an internal critic, can create a profound sense of self-doubt and inadequacy. In the context of divorce, these emotions can be particularly potent as individuals grapple with perceived failures and societal judgments.

The internal critic, a harsh and unrelenting voice, often amplifies feelings of guilt and shame. It whispers accusations of inadequacy, questioning past decisions and assigning blame. "I failed," it says, or "I should have tried harder." These self-directed criticisms can lead to a cycle of rumination, where individuals become trapped in a loop of self-reproach.

Shame, unlike guilt, which focuses on actions, attacks the core sense of self. It whispers, "I am flawed," or "I am unworthy." This emotion can lead to feelings of isolation, as individuals fear judgment from others and withdraw from social connections. The fear of being seen as a failure can create a barrier to seeking support, further perpetuating the cycle of shame.

The societal stigma surrounding divorce can exacerbate these feelings. Individuals may internalize negative judgments, believing they have deviated from societal expectations. This can lead to a sense of isolation, as they feel they are the only ones struggling with these emotions.

Acknowledging and addressing guilt and shame is crucial for healing. It requires challenging the internal critic, reframing negative self-talk, and recognizing that divorce does not define one's worth. It involves embracing self-compassion and understanding that mistakes are a part of the human experience.

Healing Shame: Reframing the Narrative

- **Name It:** "I'm feeling shame about..." Acknowledge the emotion.
- **Challenge It:** "Would I judge a friend this harshly?" Question the validity of the shame.
- **Reframe It:** "This ending doesn't define my worth." Reconstruct the narrative.

The Lies We Tell Ourselves: Distorted Perceptions

During the tumultuous period following a divorce, the mind, grappling with intense emotional pain, often constructs distorted narratives, lies that perpetuate suffering and hinder healing. These self-deceptive stories, rooted in fear and insecurity, can become powerful obstacles to recovery.

"I'll always be alone," whispers the voice of fear, painting a bleak picture of future isolation. "I'm unworthy of love," echoes the voice of shame, undermining self-esteem and creating a barrier to future connections. These narratives, while seemingly rooted in reality, are often exaggerations, distortions of the truth shaped by the trauma of loss.

These lies are not conscious fabrications; they are the mind's attempt to make sense of a chaotic and painful experience. They are echoes of past hurts, amplified by the present pain, creating a self-fulfilling prophecy of despair.

It's crucial to recognize these distorted perceptions for what they are: echoes of pain, not truths. By challenging these narratives by reframing them with compassion and understanding, individuals can begin to dismantle the barriers to healing and reclaim their sense of hope.

Exercise: Truth vs. Lie, Challenging Distortions

Lie My Pain Tells Me	Kinder Truth
"I'm unlovable."	"I am capable of love and being loved."
"I'll never recover."	"Healing takes time, but it's possible"

The Courage to Feel: Embracing Vulnerability

In a society that often equates vulnerability with weakness, the act of acknowledging and embracing one's pain during divorce is a profound act of courage. It requires a willingness to step outside the armor of stoicism and confront the raw, unfiltered emotions that accompany loss. This courage is not about being fearless but about-facing fear, sadness, and anger without denial or suppression.

To say, "These hurts, and that's okay," is to defy the pressure to project an image of unwavering strength. It is to acknowledge one's humanity and recognize that pain is an inherent part of the human experience. It is to give yourself permission to grieve, to heal, and to grow at one's own pace.

The courage to feel also involves dismantling the illusion of perfect control. It is to accept that one cannot always be "fine" and that there will be moments of vulnerability, moments of doubt, and moments of overwhelming sadness. It is important to understand that these moments are not signs of weakness but rather opportunities for growth and self-discovery.

Embracing vulnerability is not about wallowing in pain but about creating space for healing. It is about allowing oneself to experience the full spectrum of emotions, to process them, and to move forward with greater self-awareness and resilience. It is about recognizing that true strength lies not in suppressing emotions but in having the courage to feel them, to learn from them, and to emerge stronger on the other side.

Closing: The First Step Toward Healing, Recognizing the Wounds

This chapter has not offered quick fixes or simplistic solutions. Instead, it has aimed to illuminate the landscape of divorce grief to validate the complex and often conflicting emotions that arise during this tumultuous time. The primary focus has been on recognition, acknowledging the wounds inflicted by loss, and understanding the profound impact they have on the individual's emotional well-being.

Before the process of rebuilding can begin, before the scattered pieces of a shattered life can be gathered and reassembled, the pain must be seen, acknowledged, and validated. To ignore or suppress the hurt is to deny oneself the opportunity for genuine healing. It is to build a foundation on the sand, where the cracks of unresolved pain will eventually undermine any attempt at reconstruction.

Recognizing the wounds involves more than simply acknowledging the presence of pain. It requires a deep dive into the emotional landscape and a willingness to explore the anger, sadness, guilt, and shame that accompany divorce. It involves understanding the unique challenges posed by the absence of societal rituals, the burden of unspoken grief, and the distorted perceptions that perpetuate suffering.

This process of recognition is not easy. It requires courage, vulnerability, and a willingness to confront uncomfortable truths. However, it is an essential step on the path to healing. By acknowledging the wounds by giving them a voice and a name, individuals can begin to process their emotions, dismantle the barriers to recovery, and reclaim their sense of agency.

The journey ahead may seem daunting, but it is important to remember that you are not alone. You have already taken the hardest step: facing the storm, acknowledging the pain, and recognizing the wounds. And you are still standing, a testament to your resilience and your capacity for healing.

Reflection Questions: A Path to Self-Understanding

To facilitate a deeper understanding of your emotional experience during this challenging time, consider reflecting on the following questions. Remember, there are no right or wrong answers, and the purpose of these questions is to create a safe space for self-exploration and to cultivate greater self-awareness. Approach this exercise with patience and gentleness towards yourself.

- **What emotion has surprised you the most in this process?** Divorce can trigger a complex and often unexpected range of emotions. It's common to experience feelings you didn't anticipate or to find that familiar emotions arise with surprising intensity. Take a moment to consider which emotion has stood out to you in its unexpectedness. Is it a surge of anger where you expected sadness? A wave of relief amid feelings of loss? Perhaps even a feeling of empowerment or a sense of freedom you didn't foresee? Exploring this surprising emotion can reveal deeper layers of your experience and provide valuable insights into your healing process. *Aha moment: Recognizing an unexpected emotion can illuminate hidden aspects of your inner landscape and your journey.*

- **What's one way you can honor your feelings this week?** All emotions, whether pleasant or painful, deserve acknowledgment and a healthy outlet for expression. This question prompts you to identify a specific action you can take in the coming week to honor your current emotional state. This might involve dedicating time for journaling to give your thoughts and feelings a voice, engaging in a creative activity like painting or writing to express yourself non-verbally, seeking support from a trusted friend or therapist to share your burdens, or simply allowing yourself periods of quiet reflection to feel your emotions without judgment or suppression. Perhaps a long walk in nature, listening to music that resonates with your mood, or engaging in some form of physical activity would feel most supportive. Consider what form of expression or self-care would resonate most deeply with your emotional needs this week. *Aha moment: Understanding that is actively honoring your feelings, even the difficult ones, is a vital act of self-care and a step towards healing.*

- **What compassionate truth do you need to hear right now?** During times of emotional distress, we often yearn for specific messages of reassurance, validation, and support. This question invites you to identify the compassionate truth that would offer you the most comfort and strength in this moment. What words of encouragement would resonate with your heart? Do you need to hear that you are strong and capable of navigating this? That you are worthy of love and happiness? That healing takes time, and there's no need to rush. That it's okay to ask for help and lean on others? Or simply that you are not alone in this experience? Reflect on the message that would nurture your spirit and provide a sense of solace. *Aha moment: Identifying the specific compassionate truth you need to hear can provide a powerful sense of comfort, validation, and inner peace.*

Chapter 3:

Self Care – Your Beacon in the Dark

Your Lifeline in the Storm: Why Self-Care Matters During and After Divorce

Divorce, a seismic event that shatters the landscape of one's life, doesn't merely signify the legal dissolution of a marriage; it often dismantles the very scaffolding of your identity. It's an experience that can leave you feeling adrift, unmoored from the familiar shores of your existence. The loss extends far beyond the termination of a partnership; it's the unraveling of shared dreams, the erosion of a carefully constructed life, and the shattering of the image you held of yourself within that context. In its wake, you may find yourself grappling with a profound sense of hollowness, as if the person you once recognized in the mirror has been irrevocably altered, replaced by a stranger navigating unfamiliar terrain.

The emotional toll of this upheaval is not merely significant; it's often utterly exhausting. The relentless waves of grief, the constant questioning, the gnawing anxiety about the future, these forces conspire to drain your energy, leaving you feeling depleted and overwhelmed. In the midst of this emotional storm, it's tragically easy to neglect the one person who needs your care and compassion the most: you. Ironically, at the very moment you require the most tenderness and understanding, you may find yourself extending the least. This neglect is not a sign of weakness but a common response to profound trauma. It's a natural inclination to prioritize the immediate crisis and focus on survival while overlooking the long-term need for self-preservation.

This chapter is offered as a gentle, unwavering reminder that self-care is not a selfish indulgence but an essential act of survival. It's a lifeline, a beacon in the darkness, guiding you through the storm of emotions that threaten to overwhelm you. It's a recognition that you are not merely a survivor of this event but also a participant in your own healing. Right now, in the thick of this challenging transition, survival is paramount, and self-care is your most potent tool for navigating the difficult path ahead. It's about acknowledging that you are worthy of care, that your pain is valid, and that tending to your needs is not a luxury but a necessity. It's about reclaiming your agency in the face of immense loss and understanding that you have the power to nurture yourself back to wholeness, one small act of kindness at a time. It's about remembering that even in the darkest of nights, a single light can guide you home. This chapter is that light, a gentle guide to help you rediscover the strength within and to remind you that you are not alone in this journey.

Why Self-Care Feels Impossible (And Why You Must Do It Anyway)

When the foundations of your life have been shaken when your heart feels as though it has been shattered into a thousand pieces, the very notion of self-care can seem not only absurd but also utterly impossible. It's a paradoxical situation: at the very moment you need the most nurturing and compassion, you may find yourself feeling the least inclined to provide it. The sheer weight of emotional pain, the pervasive sense of loss, and the overwhelming uncertainty about the future can create a mental and emotional fog, making even the simplest acts of self-preservation seem like insurmountable tasks.

You might find yourself grappling with a barrage of self-defeating thoughts, each one a testament to the depth of your pain:

- "How can I possibly focus on eating well and preparing nutritious meals when I can barely muster the energy to get out of bed? The act of cooking, of choosing food, feels like an impossible chore, a burden I simply cannot bear. The kitchen, once a place of comfort, now feels like a battleground, and the idea of nourishing myself seems like a distant, unattainable goal."
- "Why bother with exercise, with moving my body, when I'm so numb that I feel nothing, not even the physical sensations of movement? The idea of physical exertion seems pointless, a hollow attempt to engage with a world that feels distant and unreal. My body feels heavy, unresponsive, and the thought of pushing it further seems cruel and pointless."
- "What's the point of 'me-time,' of setting aside moments for myself when I don't even recognize the person I see in the mirror? The reflection staring back at me is a stranger, a ghost of my former self, and the idea of nurturing this unfamiliar being seems futile. The concept of self-indulgence feels like a betrayal, a selfish act in the face of such profound loss."

These thoughts, these deeply ingrained beliefs, are entirely valid, understandable responses to the profound pain you are experiencing. Pain has a way of casting a long, dark shadow over everything, making even the most basic acts of self-preservation seem meaningless, like empty rituals in a world that has lost its meaning. The emotional turmoil can create a sense of apathy, a feeling of being adrift in an ocean of despair, where the concept of self-care seems like a distant shore, unreachable and irrelevant.

However, it is precisely during these moments of deep despair, when self-care feels most impossible, that it becomes most crucial. It's not about denying the pain or pretending that everything is alright. It's about acknowledging the reality of your situation, recognizing the depth of your wounds, and choosing to extend compassion to yourself in the midst of your suffering. It's about recognizing that even in the midst of chaos, you are worthy of care and that your needs are valid.

Here's the truth, offered with gentle reassurance: Self-care is the bridge between the person you were before this life-altering event and the person you are becoming. It's not about achieving a miraculous transformation overnight or about magically erasing the pain. Rather, it's about engaging in small, deliberate acts of kindness toward yourself that, over time, will help you rebuild your life and rediscover your sense of self. It's about recognizing that you are not broken beyond repair and that you have the strength to navigate this challenging journey. It's about remembering that even in the darkest of nights, a single act of kindness can ignite a spark of hope, a beacon guiding you towards healing.

The Three Pillars of Self-Care After Divorce

In the journey of healing after divorce, three fundamental pillars of self-care stand as guiding lights, offering stability and support as you navigate the turbulent waters of grief and change. These pillars, nourishing your body, soothing your mind, and feeding your soul, are not isolated practices but interconnected aspects of a holistic approach to self-care.

Nourish Your Body (Even When It Feels Like a Chore)

Your body, the vessel that carries you through life, has endured a profound trauma. The relentless stress, the sleepless nights, and the crushing weight of emotional exhaustion take a significant physical toll. While the idea of overhauling your entire lifestyle may seem overwhelming, it's crucial to acknowledge that you deserve nourishment, even in the smallest ways.

- **Eat like you love yourself.** This doesn't mean adhering to a strict diet or forcing yourself to eat elaborate meals. It means choosing foods that provide sustenance and comfort, even if it's just one healthy meal today. Consider simple, nourishing options like a warm bowl of soup, a colorful salad, or a smoothie packed with fruits and vegetables. Small, consistent acts of nourishing your body can make a significant difference in your overall well-being, providing the energy you need to navigate each day. Remember, even small steps are powerful.
- **Move in ways that feel good.** Exercise doesn't have to be a grueling workout at the gym. It can be a gentle walk in nature, a few minutes of stretching or dancing freely in your living room to your favorite music. Movement helps release pent-up grief and tension, promoting both physical and emotional

well-being. Listen to your body and choose activities that bring you a sense of ease and comfort. Even a short walk around the block can provide a sense of grounding and connection to the present moment.

- **Rest without guilt.** Sleep when you can, and don't hesitate to nap if you need to. Healing is exhausting work, and your body requires rest to recover. Allow yourself to prioritize sleep without feeling guilty or unproductive. Create a calming bedtime routine, such as reading a book or listening to soothing music, to promote restful sleep. Remember, rest is not a luxury but a necessity for healing.

2. Soothe Your Mind (Because It's Been Through Enough)

Your mind, the battlefield of regrets, anger, and fear of the future, needs a respite from the relentless noise of negative thoughts. Self-care, in this context, means creating moments of peace and tranquility, giving your mind a chance to rest and recover.

- **Breathe.** Take five deep breaths right now. Inhale peace, exhale pain. This simple act can help calm your nervous system and create a sense of grounding. Practice deep breathing exercises throughout the day, especially during moments of stress or anxiety.
- **Limit triggers.** It's perfectly acceptable to mute social media, avoid certain places, or say no to conversations that drain you. Protect your mental space and minimize exposure to potential triggers. Identify the people, places, and things that trigger negative emotions, and create boundaries to protect your peace.

- **Try mindfulness.** Even five minutes of meditation or journaling can create a space between you and the pain, allowing you to observe your thoughts without judgment and find moments of stillness. Consider using guided meditation apps or journaling prompts to cultivate mindfulness and self-awareness.

3. Feed Your Soul (Rediscovering What Brings You Joy)

Divorce can cast a pall over the world, making everything seem colorless and devoid of joy. However, beauty still exists, and you are still a part of it. Self-care, in this aspect, means intentionally reconnecting with the things that bring you joy and nourish your soul.

- **Reconnect with what you love.** Rediscover a forgotten hobby, listen to music that lifts your spirits, or immerse yourself in a book that provides comfort. Reclaim the activities that bring you joy and remind you of your passions. Allow yourself to indulge in these activities without guilt or reservation.
- **Spend time in nature.** Sunlight, fresh air, the sound of leaves rustling, these are small but powerful healers. Allow yourself to be surrounded by the beauty and tranquility of nature. Even a short walk in a park or a visit to a botanical garden can provide a sense of calm and connection to the natural world.
- **Create something.** Write, paint, cook, garden, or engage in any creative activity that allows you to express yourself. Making something new reminds you that you are not broken beyond repair and that you have the capacity to create beauty and meaning

in your life. Allow yourself to experiment with different forms of creative expression, and don't be afraid to make mistakes.

These three pillars of self-care are not about achieving perfection but about extending compassion to yourself during a challenging time. They are about recognizing your needs, honoring your emotions, and taking small steps toward healing.

Self-Care Is Resistance

In a world that often expects you to "move on" quickly, suppress your emotions and pretend that everything is fine, choosing self-care is an act of defiance. It's a powerful declaration:

- "I will not abandon myself."
- "I will not rush this grief."
- "I will heal in my own time, in my own way."

There will be days when even the smallest act of self-care feels impossibly difficult. On those days, simply do this:

- Drink a glass of water, nourishing your body with life-giving hydration.
- Step outside for one minute, allowing the fresh air and sunlight to revitalize your spirit.
- Tell yourself, "This is hard, but I'm still here." Affirm your resilience and your ability to endure.

That's enough. That's a victory.

The Lies We Tell Ourselves (And How to Counter Them)

Divorce, in its aftermath, often unleashes a torrent of self-doubt, a relentless chorus of negative self-talk that can erode your sense of worth and hinder your healing journey. These self-defeating thoughts, while seemingly rooted in reality, are often distorted reflections of your pain, whispers of fear and insecurity that seek to define your future.

"I failed," the internal critic whispers, casting a shadow of inadequacy over your past. "I'll never love again," fear proclaims, painting a bleak picture of future loneliness. "I don't deserve happiness," shame asserts, undermining your belief in your own inherent worth. These pronouncements, while deeply felt, are not objective truths; they are wounds speaking, echoes of pain that distort your perception of reality.

Challenging these lies requires a conscious and deliberate effort, a gentle but firm act of self-reclamation. It involves reframing your narrative replacing self-defeating thoughts with compassionate affirmations that acknowledge your strength and resilience.

- "I survived something incredibly hard. That's strength, not failure." This affirmation acknowledges your capacity to endure your ability to navigate immense challenges. It reframes the experience of divorce not as a sign of weakness but as a testament to your inner fortitude.
- "My capacity to love isn't gone; it's just healing." This affirmation offers hope for future connections, reminding you that your heart, though wounded, retains its capacity for love. It acknowledges the

healing process, emphasizing that time and self-compassion are essential for rebuilding trust and opening yourself to new relationships.

- "Happiness isn't a reward for being perfect. It's my birthright." This affirmation challenges the notion that happiness is contingent on external validation or flawless behavior. It asserts your inherent right to joy, regardless of past mistakes or perceived shortcomings.

These counter-narratives are not mere platitudes; they are tools for reclaiming your agency and rewriting the story of your life.

They are reminders that you are not defined by your divorce, that you are capable of healing, and that you deserve happiness. By consistently challenging the lies you tell yourself, you can begin to dismantle the barriers to recovery and embrace a future filled with hope and self-compassion.

Building a Self-Care Toolkit (Practical Strategies for Dark Days)

The emotional landscape of divorce is often unpredictable, marked by sudden storms of grief that can leave you feeling overwhelmed and adrift. During these dark days, having a pre-prepared self-care toolkit can act as a steady anchor, a tangible reminder that you possess the resources to navigate these turbulent waters. This toolkit is not a luxury but a necessity, a compassionate act of self-preservation.

Creating this toolkit is a deeply personal endeavor, requiring introspection and a willingness to identify what truly soothes and comforts you. It's about assembling a collection of strategies and items that resonate with your unique needs, creating a personalized arsenal of self-soothing techniques.

- **Comfort Playlist:** Beyond just compiling favorite songs, consider curating a playlist that reflects the emotional journey of healing. Include songs that acknowledge the pain but also uplift and inspire resilience. Think of it as a sonic journey through your emotions, providing a sense of companionship during moments of solitude.

- **Emergency Self-Soothe Kit:** This kit should engage multiple senses, providing a multi-layered approach to comfort. Include items like a soft, weighted blanket for grounding, essential oils with calming scents like lavender or chamomile, a small journal for expressive writing, or a collection of comforting photographs. Consider including tactile items like a smooth stone or a soft piece of fabric.

- **Safe People List:** This list is more than just names and numbers. It's a carefully selected group of individuals who offer unconditional support, non-judgmental listening, and a safe space for vulnerability. Include individuals who understand the complexities of grief and who will simply be present with you without offering unsolicited advice or minimizing your pain.

This toolkit is a living document, evolving as you navigate your healing journey. Regularly revisit and update its contents, adding new strategies and removing those that no longer serve you. Experiment with different techniques, exploring what truly brings you comfort and peace. Remember, this toolkit is a testament to your commitment to self-care, a tangible expression of your belief in your own capacity to heal.

The Power of Small Rituals (Anchors in the Chaos)

In the disorienting aftermath of divorce, when routines are shattered, and the familiar landscape of life feels irrevocably altered, small, intentional rituals can serve as powerful anchors, providing a sense of stability and grounding amidst the chaos. These rituals, though seemingly insignificant, offer a sense of control and predictability, creating moments of peace and connection to oneself during a time of immense upheaval.

These rituals don't have to be grand or elaborate; they are most effective when they are simple, consistent, and deeply personal. They are acts of self-care woven into the fabric of daily life, offering moments of respite and reflection.

- **Light a candle with the intention: "This light is for me."** This simple act transforms a mundane activity into a moment of self-dedication. As the flame flickers, it serves as a visual reminder of your inner light, your resilience, and your commitment to self-nurturing. It creates a sacred space, a moment of stillness in the midst of the storm.
- **Every morning, say one thing you're grateful for , even if it's just "I woke up."** This practice shifts the focus from what has been lost to what remains. It cultivates a sense of gratitude, even in the

face of immense pain. It's a reminder that even in the darkest of times, there are still small moments of beauty and blessings to be found.

- **End the day by placing a hand over your heart and whispering, "You're doing your best."** This ritual is an act of self-compassion; a gentle acknowledgment of the challenges faced throughout the day. It validates your efforts, reminding you that you are doing your best, even when it doesn't feel like enough. It's a moment of tender self-acceptance.

These rituals, when practiced consistently, create a sense of continuity and stability, providing a framework for navigating the unpredictable waves of grief. They are small acts of defiance against the chaos, reclaiming moments of peace and connection to oneself. They are gentle reminders that even amidst the storm, you are worthy of care and compassion.

When Self-Care Feels Like Too Much (And That's Okay)

There will inevitably be days during the healing process when even the most basic acts of self-care feel insurmountable. When the weight of grief presses down with unbearable heaviness, and even the act of breathing feels like a monumental effort, it's crucial to remember that this is a valid and understandable experience. It's okay to acknowledge that self-care, at times, can feel like an impossible task.

In these moments, it's essential to release the pressure to perform self-care perfectly and instead prioritize gentle self-compassion.

- **Ask for help.** Reaching out for support is not a sign of weakness but a testament to your strength. Seek assistance from a therapist, a support group, or even a trusted friend or family member. If in-person support is unavailable, online communities or helplines can offer connection and understanding.
- **Scale back.** If the self-care activities you've planned feel overwhelming, scale them back to the bare minimum. Instead of a 30-minute walk, try 30 seconds of stretching. Instead of a full meal, focus on hydrating with a glass of water. Any small act of self-care is a victory.
- **Surrender.** Healing is not a linear process. There will be moments of regression, moments when you feel like you're falling apart. In these moments, allow yourself to surrender to the pain, to release the pressure to be strong. Know that you have the resilience to piece yourself back together when you're ready.

Remember, self-care is not about achieving perfection or maintaining a flawless facade. It's about extending compassion to yourself during moments of vulnerability. It's about acknowledging your limitations and honoring your needs. It's about understanding that healing takes time and that it's okay to take breaks along the way.

The Quiet Rebellion of Choosing Yourself

Divorce, in its disruptive force, can often leave you feeling disempowered, as if control over your own life has been wrested away. However, within the realm of self-care lies a quiet but profound rebellion, a reclaiming of agency and a reassertion of your inherent worth. Every deliberate act of self-care, no matter how small, is a powerful declaration of self-preservation and a refusal to be defined by loss.

This rebellion is not loud or aggressive; it is a gentle but unwavering commitment to prioritizing your own well-being. It is about recognizing that your needs matter, that your emotions are valid, and that you deserve to be treated with kindness and compassion, especially by yourself.

- **Saying no to what drains you is power.** In the aftermath of divorce, you may find yourself bombarded with demands and expectations from others. Setting boundaries and refusing to engage in activities or relationships that deplete your energy is an act of self-preservation. It is a reclaiming of your time and your emotional resources.
- **Prioritizing your needs is power.** This is not about selfishness; it is about self-respect. It is about recognizing that your well-being is essential for your healing journey. It is about giving yourself permission to prioritize rest, nourishment, and emotional support.
- **Believing in your own worth is power.** Divorce can erode your sense of self-worth, leaving you questioning your value and your lovability. However, choosing self-care is an act of affirming your inherent worth. It is a declaration that you deserve happiness, healing, and a fulfilling life.

This quiet rebellion is not about fighting against the past; it is about building a future defined by self-compassion and resilience. It is about rewriting your story, reclaiming your narrative, and creating a life that reflects your true values and desires. It is a journey of empowerment, a process of rediscovering your strength and your capacity for joy.

You Are Worth the Effort

Self-care isn't about achieving a state of perfection or being "fixed." It's about being tended to by you, for you. It's about acknowledging your needs, honoring your emotions, and providing yourself with the care and compassion you deserve.

Because somewhere beneath the layers of grief, fear, and exhaustion, you still exist. The person who is fighting to heal, rebuild, and rediscover joy deserves every ounce of kindness and compassion you can muster. One small act of care at a time, one gentle step toward healing. You are worth the effort. You are worth the love. You are worth the care. You are worth it all.

Closing: The Light Will Find You

Healing from divorce is not about reaching a definitive finish line, a point where all pain magically disappears, and life is once again perfect. Instead, it is a continuous journey of growth, adaptation, and self-discovery. It's about learning to carry your pain with tenderness and acceptance rather than with resentment and bitterness. It's about acknowledging that the scars of the past will remain, but they will eventually fade, becoming reminders of your strength and resilience.

There will inevitably be days when the light of hope feels distant and when the darkness of grief seems to overwhelm you. On these days, it's crucial to remember that the light has not vanished; it is simply obscured. It's still there, waiting to be rediscovered, patiently waiting for you to find your way back to it.

This light can manifest in unexpected ways: in the warmth of a comforting cup of tea, in the quiet solitude of an early morning, in the gentle beauty of a sunset, in the unwavering support of a friend, or in the quiet courage it takes to simply keep going. It is found in the small acts of self-care, in the moments of self-compassion, and in the persistent belief in your own capacity for healing.

You are not alone in this journey. Many have walked this path before you, and many will walk it after you. You are part of a community of resilience, a testament to the enduring human spirit. And you will find your way back to yourself, to a place of wholeness and joy. It may take time, it may require patience, but the light will find you. Trust in your strength, embrace your vulnerability, and allow yourself to heal at your own pace.

Reflection Questions: A Path to Self-Understanding

To deepen your understanding of self-care and to personalize its application in your healing journey, consider reflecting on the following questions. There are no right or wrong answers; the goal is to create a space for honest self-exploration and to cultivate a greater sense of self-awareness. Allow yourself time and space to answer these questions with compassion and gentleness.

- **What emotion has surprised you the most in this process?** Divorce often evokes a complex and sometimes unexpected range of emotions. You may find yourself experiencing feelings you didn't anticipate or feeling them with an intensity that surprises you. This question invites you to acknowledge these unexpected emotions, to explore their origins, and to accept them as a valid part of your experience. *Aha moment: Recognizing an unexpected emotion can illuminate hidden aspects of your inner landscape and your journey.*

- **What's one way you can honor your feelings this week?** Feelings, whether pleasant or painful, deserve acknowledgment and expression. This question encourages you to identify a concrete action you can take to honor your emotional landscape. This might involve journaling, creative expression, talking to a trusted friend, or simply allowing yourself time and space to feel without judgment. *Aha moment: Understanding that was actively honoring your feelings, even the difficult ones, is a vital act of self-care and a step towards healing.*

- **What compassionate truth do you need to hear right now?** During times of emotional distress, we often need to hear specific messages of reassurance and support. This question prompts you to identify the compassionate truth that would provide comfort and validation. It might be a reminder of your strength, your worthiness, or your capacity for healing. *Aha moment: Identifying the specific compassionate truth you need to hear can provide a powerful sense of comfort, validation, and inner peace.*

- **What self-care practice feels most challenging for you right now, and why?** Self-care, while essential, can sometimes feel difficult or even impossible to prioritize, especially when you're navigating the complexities of divorce. This question encourages you to explore the barriers that may be preventing you from engaging in self-care, whether they are practical, such as lack of time or resources. Emotional, such as feeling undeserving or overwhelmed, or mental, such as negative self-talk or resistance. By identifying these challenges, you can begin to address them with greater awareness and self-compassion, perhaps finding small, manageable ways to overcome them. *Aha moment: Recognizing the specific obstacles that make self-care difficult for you can help you approach them with more understanding and find creative solutions.*

- **What small act of kindness can you offer yourself today?** Self-compassion is a cornerstone of healing, especially during times of vulnerability and pain. This question invites you to consider a tangible act of kindness you can extend to yourself at this very moment. It might be something as simple as taking a few deep breaths, drinking a glass of water, stepping outside for some fresh air, offering yourself gentle and encouraging words, or allowing yourself a few minutes of rest without guilt. Even the smallest gestures of self-compassion can make a significant difference in your overall well-being. *Aha moment: Recognizing that you deserve kindness and actively offering yourself a small act of care can provide immediate comfort and support.*

- **What is one strength you have discovered in yourself during this process?** Even in the midst of pain and loss, divorce can unexpectedly reveal hidden strengths and resilience you might not have known you possessed. This question encourages you to acknowledge your inner fortitude and recognize the specific qualities that have helped you navigate this challenging experience. Perhaps you've discovered a newfound independence, a deeper sense of self-reliance, or an unexpected wellspring of courage. Celebrating these strengths, no matter how small they might seem, can foster a sense of empowerment and hope as you continue your healing journey. *Aha moment: Identifying and acknowledging a personal strength you've discovered during this time can build your confidence and remind you of your inner resources.*

Chapter 4:

Sharing Your Burden

The Weight You Were Never Meant to Carry Alone

Divorce, in its essence, is a profoundly disruptive and often isolating experience. It's a journey that can leave you feeling adrift in a sea of unfamiliar emotions and circumstances. Even when surrounded by others, you may find yourself enveloped in a deep sense of aloneness, as if an invisible barrier separates you from the world. It can feel as though no one could truly comprehend the unique and intense combination of grief, anger, confusion, and fear that you're navigating. The familiar landmarks of your life, routines, relationships, and even your sense of self, may have shifted or disappeared, leaving you feeling lost and disoriented.

This isolation is a common and understandable response to the profound loss and upheaval that divorce brings. It can stem from various sources, including the shattering of shared routines and dreams, the loss of a primary confidant, the fear of judgment or misunderstanding, and the sheer exhaustion of processing the emotional fallout. The weight of these burdens can create a sense of being trapped in a solitary struggle, amplifying feelings of loneliness and despair.

But here's what you must remember, what you must hold onto with unwavering conviction: Your pain is valid, and it is not yours to bear in silence. You are not alone in this experience, and seeking connection is not a sign of weakness or inadequacy; it's a fundamental human need and a crucial step towards healing.

There's an old saying, a simple yet powerful truth that resonates across cultures and generations: "A problem shared is a problem halved." This isn't a magical solution that will instantly erase your hurt or make the pain disappear. It doesn't promise to provide immediate relief from the emotional turmoil. However, it does mean that the crushing weight of solitude, the debilitating belief that you must suffer in silence, that no one could possibly understand your experience, can begin to lift when you allow others to witness your struggle and offer support. Sharing your burden opens the door to connection, empathy, and understanding, which are essential components of the healing process. It's about acknowledging that you are not meant to navigate this journey alone and that seeking support is an act of strength and self-care.

The Myth of "I Should Handle This Alone"

One of the most pervasive and insidious lies that grief whispers in the aftermath of divorce is the myth of self-sufficiency: the deeply ingrained belief that you must shoulder this immense burden alone, that seeking help is a sign of weakness or inadequacy. This myth can be particularly compelling in a culture that often glorifies independence and stoicism, where vulnerability is sometimes perceived as a flaw. It can lead to a self-imposed isolation that hinders the healing process.

Why We Isolate Ourselves in Pain: The Roots of Self-Reliance

After a divorce, you might find yourself constructing elaborate justifications for your isolation, building a fortress of self-reliance to protect yourself from perceived vulnerability. These thoughts, while seemingly logical and protective, are often rooted in fear, insecurity, and deeply ingrained beliefs about strength and independence.

You might tell yourself:

- "I don't want to burden anyone with my problems. Everyone else has their own struggles; I shouldn't add to their load. I need to be strong for them."
- "People will judge me for 'failing' at my marriage. They'll think I'm weak or incapable, and I can't bear that shame."
- "No one really understands what I'm going through. My experience is unique, and no one can truly empathize with the depth of my pain."

These thoughts are natural defense mechanisms. They are attempts to protect yourself from perceived judgment, rejection, or further hurt. However, they are also distortions of reality, lies that grief tells you to keep you isolated.

The Truth: Debunking the Myths of Isolation

The truth is far different, and it's essential to embrace this counter-narrative:

- **Vulnerability is not weakness. It takes immense courage to say, "I'm not okay."** Acknowledging your pain and seeking support is not a sign of inadequacy; it is a testament to your strength and self-awareness.
- **Asking for help is not selfish. It is an act of self-respect.** Reaching out for support is not a burden on others; it is an invitation to connect and build stronger relationships.
- **You are not a failure. You are a person navigating profound loss, and that deserves compassion.** Divorce is not a reflection of your worth. You deserve kindness and understanding.

By recognizing the falsity of the "I should handle this alone" myth, you can begin to dismantle the barriers to connection and embrace the healing power of shared experience.

Finding Your People, The Art of Selective Vulnerability

While sharing your burden is undeniably crucial for healing and reconnecting with your humanity, it's equally, if not more, important to recognize that not everyone is equipped or deserving of bearing witness to your pain. The concept of "selective vulnerability" emphasizes the importance of discernment, a careful and considered approach to choosing whom to confide in and entrust with the delicate intricacies of your emotional journey. It's about exercising agency to protect your heart.

Vulnerability, the courageous act of opening yourself up and sharing your authentic feelings, is a powerful force for forging deep connections and facilitating profound healing. However, it's a force that requires a safe and nurturing environment and a foundation of unwavering trust. Indiscriminate vulnerability, sharing your pain with anyone and everyone who crosses your path, can leave you feeling exposed, emotionally drained, and potentially retraumatized by misunderstanding or judgment.

Therefore, "finding your people" becomes an essential and empowering aspect of self-care during and after the tumultuous period of divorce. It's not about building walls but about cultivating a circle of support that actively nurtures your healing and prioritizes your emotional well-being. This involves:

- **Identifying Safe People:** These are the individuals in your life who have consistently demonstrated empathy, compassion, and an unwavering willingness to listen without judgment or interruption. They are the ones who create a space where you feel genuinely heard, deeply validated, and unconditionally accepted. They are reliable in respecting your boundaries, allowing you to share at your own pace, and honoring the sanctity of your vulnerability.

- **Recognizing Unsafe People:** Conversely, it's equally important to recognize those individuals who may, either inadvertently or intentionally, cause further harm to your already tender heart. These may be people who dismiss your pain as trivial, offer unsolicited advice that feels invalidating, engage in gossip or judgment of you or your ex-partner, or have a tendency to make your experience about themselves, draining your emotional energy and leaving you feeling unheard. It's crucial to establish firm boundaries with these individuals, not out of malice but out of a fierce commitment to protecting your own peace and emotional resilience.

The art of selective vulnerability is, at its core, an act of self-empowerment. It's about recognizing that you possess the inherent right to choose who has access to the sacred space of your emotional world. It's about prioritizing your own well-being and actively curating a supportive network that fosters genuine healing and sustainable growth. It's about understanding that vulnerability, while a source of immense strength and connection, needs to be exercised with wisdom, discernment, and a profound respect for your own heart's journey.

Who to Turn To (And Who to Avoid)

Safe People	Unsafe People
Friends who listen without fixing	Those who dismiss your pain ("Just move on!")
Support groups with shared experiences	People who gossip or judge
Therapists or counselors	Those who make it about themselves

Exercise: Make a shortlist of 2-3 people you trust. Next to each name, write one way they've supported you before.

How to Ask for Help (When You Hate Asking)

- "I'm struggling. Can I talk to you?"
- "I don't need advice, just someone to listen."
- "Can we meet for coffee? I could use a friend right now."
- You don't have to perform strength. My real strength is saying, "I need you."

The Power of Shared Stories, Support Groups & Therapy

Sometimes, in the aftermath of divorce, the most profound connections and the deepest healing can emerge from sharing your story with individuals who are, in many ways, strangers to your past. Support groups and therapy offer unique opportunities for connection, understanding, and healing, providing a space where you can process your experience without the weight of pre-existing relationships or expectations.

Why Talking to Strangers Can Be Easier: The Benefits of Neutrality and Shared Experience

There are several compelling reasons why sharing your journey with strangers in a structured setting can be incredibly beneficial:

- **Speak without fear of judgment:** Within the safe confines of a support group or therapy session, you are typically surrounded by individuals who have a shared understanding of your pain. This fosters an environment of empathy and acceptance, allowing you to express your vulnerability without fear of being judged or misunderstood.

- **Hear others say, "Me too", a powerful antidote to shame:** Discovering that your experiences, emotions, and challenges are not unique can be profoundly validating. Hearing others articulate similar struggles can shatter the illusion of isolation, dispel feelings of shame, and create a powerful sense of belonging. The shared "Me too" is a potent reminder that you are not alone in your journey.

- **Gain tools from those further along in healing:** Support groups often include individuals at various stages of the healing process. Those who have navigated similar terrain and emerged with greater strength and resilience can offer invaluable insights, practical advice, and a tangible sense of hope for the future. They serve as living proof that healing is possible.

These forms of support provide a unique blend of community and guidance, offering both a sense of belonging and practical strategies for navigating the complexities of divorce. They are spaces where shared stories become a source of strength, empowering individuals to reclaim their lives and move towards a brighter future.

Navigating Well-Meaning (But Painful) Comments

Even the most well-intentioned individuals in your life, friends, family members, colleagues, may, in their attempts to offer support, inadvertently make comments that are hurtful, insensitive, or simply unhelpful. This often stems from a lack of understanding of the complexities of divorce, discomfort with expressions of grief, or a well-meaning but misguided desire to offer unsolicited advice or fix the situation. Learning how to navigate these situations with grace, assertiveness, and a strong sense of self-preservation is crucial for protecting your emotional well-being and maintaining your boundaries during the healing process.

The key is to remember that you are not responsible for managing other people's discomfort or lack of understanding. Your priority is your own emotional health. When faced with a painful or unhelpful comment, you have the right to respond in a way that feels authentic and protective. This might involve:

- **Setting boundaries:** It's okay to politely but firmly communicate that a particular comment or line of conversation is not helpful or appropriate.
- **Redirecting the conversation:** You can gently steer the discussion towards a more supportive topic or activity.
- **Expressing your needs:** Clearly articulate what kind of support you need, whether it's simply a listening ear or a break from the conversation.

It's also important to remember that you don't owe anyone a performance of "being okay." You are allowed to express your emotions, acknowledge your pain, and set boundaries that protect your peace, even if it makes others uncomfortable.

Even loved ones say the wrong things. How to handle:

Comment	What They Mean	How to Respond
"You're better off!"	They want to cheer you up.	"I know you mean well, but I'm allowed to grieve."
"How could they do this to you?"	They're angry on your behalf.	"I'm not ready to talk about blame yet."
"Just stay busy!"	They're uncomfortable with sadness.	"I need to feel this to heal."

Remember: You don't owe anyone a performance of "being okay."

When Sharing Feels Too Hard, Alternative Outlets

It's a common human experience to sometimes find the act of sharing our thoughts, feelings, and experiences incredibly difficult. Whether it stems from vulnerability, fear of judgment, past negative experiences, or a simple desire for privacy, the pressure to open up can feel overwhelming. In these moments, forcing ourselves to share before we're ready can be counterproductive and even damaging to our well-being. Thankfully, there are numerous alternative outlets we can explore to process our inner world without the immediate need for direct disclosure.

One powerful avenue is journaling or writing. Putting pen to paper (or fingers to keyboard) allows us to externalize our thoughts and emotions in a safe and private space. This can provide clarity, help us identify patterns, and offer a sense of release without the need for an audience. If words feel inadequate, consider writing letters you never intend to send, letters to an ex, to a past version of yourself, or even to the pain itself. The act of writing can be incredibly cathartic, allowing you to express feelings without the pressure of delivery or response. Different forms of writing, such as free-writing, poetry, or even creating fictional narratives, can cater to various needs and preferences.

Creative expression offers another valuable outlet. Engaging in activities like painting, drawing, sculpting, playing music, singing, or dancing can be incredibly therapeutic. These mediums allow us to communicate and express feelings that words might fail to capture. Consider creating a grief playlist that resonates with your emotions or painting your feelings using colors and shapes to convey what words cannot. The focus shifts from verbal articulation to a more visceral and embodied form of expression, which can be deeply cathartic.

For those seeking guidance and support without the pressure of sharing with loved ones, connecting with a trusted professional such as a therapist or counselor can be immensely beneficial. These individuals are trained to provide a safe and confidential space to explore our thoughts and feelings at our own pace. They can offer tools and strategies for coping and help us build the confidence to share when and if we feel ready.

Engaging in physical activity can also serve as a powerful emotional release. Exercise, whether it's running, swimming, yoga, or simply going for a walk, can help reduce stress hormones and boost mood. Beyond general exercise, consider more direct forms of physical release when overwhelmed. Screaming into a pillow, punching a mattress, or taking a rage walk can be incredibly effective in releasing pent-up frustration and anger in a safe and controlled manner.

Practicing mindfulness and meditation can help us become more aware of our thoughts and feelings without judgment. This can create a sense of inner space and allow us to observe our experiences without feeling overwhelmed by the need to share them. These practices can foster self-compassion and acceptance, making the eventual act of sharing feel less daunting.

Finally, while direct sharing might be challenging, connecting with online communities or support groups focused on specific interests or experiences can offer a sense of belonging and understanding. Observing others share their stories and offering anonymous support can be a gentle way to engage without the immediate pressure of revealing personal details. However, it's crucial to exercise caution and ensure these online spaces are safe and supportive.

Ultimately, finding alternative outlets when sharing feels too hard is about honoring our own needs and finding healthy ways to process our inner world. Your feelings deserve expression, even if no one else hears them. It's a testament to self-awareness and a step towards eventual well-being. Remember that these alternatives are not replacements for genuine connection but rather valuable tools to navigate moments when vulnerability feels overwhelming, paving the way for healthier sharing when the time is right.

The Sacred Act of Letting Others Love You

There's a profound and often challenging act in allowing ourselves to be loved. In a world that often emphasizes independence and self-reliance, the vulnerability inherent in opening our hearts to receive care and affection can feel daunting. Yet, within this very act lies a sacredness, a recognition of our shared humanity and the deep need for connection. Letting others love you isn't passive; it's an active choice to dismantle the walls we've built and permit the warmth of another's heart to touch our own.

Why is it so difficult for many of us to fully embrace the love offered? Perhaps past hurts have left us wary, creating a protective barrier against future pain. Maybe ingrained beliefs of unworthiness whisper doubts in our ears, making it hard to believe we deserve such kindness. Fear of vulnerability can also play a significant role, as allowing someone to truly see and care for us requires us to lower our defenses and risk potential hurt. Sometimes, a strong sense of self-sufficiency can make us feel like we should handle everything on our own, inadvertently pushing away the very support we need.

However, the act of letting others love you is sacred because it acknowledges our inherent worthiness and our interconnectedness. It's an invitation for healing to begin. Healing happens in moments like these: when a friend sits with you in comfortable silence, offering their presence as a silent testament to their care; when a support group member nods in understanding as you cry, validating your pain without judgment; when a therapist gently reflects,

"That must have been so hard," acknowledging the weight of your experience.

These seemingly small gestures are the threads that weave a tapestry of support and healing. They remind us that we are not alone in our struggles and that others are willing to share our burdens. As mentioned, these are the angels the book's title promises, not mythical beings, but ordinary people who help carry your pain when it's too heavy. They are the friends who offer a listening ear, the family members who provide unwavering support, unplanned occurrences that manifest compassion and love, the partners who offer comfort and understanding, and even the professionals who guide us through our darkest times.

Allowing ourselves to be loved fosters deeper connections and strengthens our relationships. It creates a reciprocal flow of care, where giving and receiving become intertwined. When we open ourselves to love, we not only benefit from the support and comfort it provides, but we also give the gift of allowing others to express their compassion and empathy. This act of receiving can be just as meaningful for the giver as it is for the receiver.

Ultimately, embracing the love offered by others is an act of courage and self-compassion. It's recognizing our vulnerability as a strength and understanding that we don't have to navigate life's challenges entirely on our own. By letting others in, by allowing them to offer their love and support, we create space for healing, growth, and a deeper sense of belonging in the world. It is in these moments of shared humanity that we truly experience the sacred power of love in its purest form.

Closing: You Are Allowed to Need People

It's a fundamental truth of the human experience that we are not meant to navigate life in complete isolation. Connection, support, and the ability to lean on others are essential for our well-being and growth. Yet, somewhere along the way, you may have learned that needing help is shameful. This societal conditioning can lead us to believe that vulnerability is a weakness and that true strength lies in unwavering independence. But here's a vital shift in perspective:

Asking for help isn't a sign that you're broken. It's proof that you're fighting to put yourself back together. In moments of struggle, reaching out is not an admission of failure but rather an act of courage and resilience. It demonstrates a willingness to confront challenges and a proactive approach to healing and growth. It takes strength to acknowledge our limitations and to trust others enough to seek their support.

The journey of life, with its inevitable ups and downs, can sometimes feel isolating. The road ahead will have lonely stretches. There will be moments of doubt, pain, and uncertainty where the weight of our experiences feels overwhelming. But remember this: you need never walk it entirely alone. There are people in your life – friends, family, partners, mentors, and even professionals – who are willing and able to offer support, understanding, and a helping hand. Allowing them to be there for you is not a burden on them but rather an opportunity to strengthen bonds and experience the beauty of human connection.

You are inherently worthy of love, support, and care. Needing people is not a flaw in your character; it's a testament to your humanity. Embracing this truth can liberate you from the pressure to always be strong and self-sufficient. It allows you to tap into a network of support that can provide comfort, guidance, and a sense of belonging. You are allowed to have moments of vulnerability, moments where you need to lean on others. In fact, these moments can be powerful catalysts for healing and growth. Embrace the connections in your life, allow yourself to be supported, and remember that needing people is not a sign of weakness but a testament to the strength of the human spirit and our innate desire for connection.

The road ahead will have lonely stretches. But you need never walk it entirely alone.

Reflection Questions: A Path to Self-Understanding

The journey to understanding ourselves is a lifelong exploration, often paved with moments of quiet introspection. Reflection questions serve as valuable tools on this path, guiding us to delve deeper into our thoughts, feelings, and experiences. To truly benefit from these prompts, take a quiet moment with these questions. Find a space where you can be free from distractions and allow your thoughts to flow without judgment. Remember, there are no right or wrong answers, only your truth. Embrace the process of self-discovery, knowing that each answer, no matter how small or profound, contributes to a richer understanding of who you are.

Let's begin this inward journey with the following questions:

Who in my life has made me feel truly heard in the past? How can I reach out to them now? This question invites us to reflect on past positive connections, identifying individuals who have offered genuine validation and understanding – those who truly listened without interrupting, judging, or immediately offering solutions. Consider what qualities made you feel heard by these individuals. How did they make you feel valued and understood? Reaching out to these people, even with a simple message, can reinforce those supportive bonds and serve as a powerful reminder that you are not alone. It's a proactive and courageous step towards building and nurturing a stronger network of care during this time. Aha moment: *Recognizing the importance of supportive connections and taking the initiative to reach out can bring comfort and strengthen your sense of belonging.*

What fears come up when I think about sharing my pain with others? Are these fears based on facts or assumptions? Examining our fears around vulnerability is crucial. Often, these fears – such as fear of judgment, of burdening others, of being misunderstood, or of not being taken seriously – are rooted in past experiences or assumptions rather than current realities. By honestly assessing the basis of these anxieties, questioning their validity, and considering if they are truly reflective of your present support system, we can begin to challenge limiting beliefs and open ourselves to the possibility of receiving the very support and understanding we need. Consider if past negative experiences are coloring your current perceptions and if there are individuals in your life now who might offer a different, more supportive response. Aha moment: *Gaining awareness of the specific fears that hinder you from sharing your pain and questioning their validity can create an opening for seeking support.*

If I could describe my emotional state in one word today, what would it be? Where do I feel that emotion in my body? This question encourages present-moment awareness and highlights the important link between our emotions and physical sensations. Identifying your primary emotional state with a single word – perhaps "sad," "anxious," "hopeful," "frustrated," or "calm" – can provide a concise snapshot of your current well-being. Then, by noticing where you physically feel that emotion in your body – a tightness in your chest, a knot in your stomach, a lightness in your head – you can gain valuable insights into how your emotions are manifesting physically and connect with your feelings on a deeper, more embodied level. This awareness can also be a gentle reminder to offer yourself care and attention in the areas where you are feeling the most impact. Aha moment: *Connecting your emotional state with physical sensations can provide a deeper understanding of your present experience and the need for self-care.*

What's one small way I can practice asking for help this week? Asking for help can be challenging, especially when we are used to being independent or feel like we should be able to handle everything on our own. However, reaching out for support is a vital aspect of self-care and a sign of strength, not weakness. This question prompts us to identify one manageable step we can take in the coming week to practice this skill. This could be as simple as texting a friend to ask how their day is going, joining an online support group to connect with others who understand, asking a neighbor for a small favor, or even taking the step to book a therapy session. Starting small can build confidence and make it easier to seek support when you truly need it, reminding you that you don't have to carry all the burdens alone. Aha moment: *Identifying a small,* *actionable step towards asking for help can empower you to seek support and build confidence in reaching out.*

When have I been there for someone else in their pain? How can I offer myself the same compassion I've given to others? Reflecting on our own capacity for empathy and support can be incredibly powerful. We often extend kindness, understanding, and patience to others who are struggling more readily than we do to ourselves. Think about a time when you were there for someone else in their pain – how did you offer comfort? What words did you use? What actions did you take? This question encourages us to turn that same compassion inward, offering ourselves the same grace, understanding, and gentle support that we would readily give to a friend in need. Recognizing our own ability to be compassionate caregivers can be a powerful reminder to extend that same kindness to ourselves during our own difficult times. Aha moment: *Recognizing your own capacity for compassion towards others can inspire you to offer that same kindness and understanding to yourself.*

Finally, consider this **Journal Prompt**:

"If my heart could speak freely to someone safe, it would say..."

This prompt provides a safe and private opportunity for unfiltered emotional expression. Imagine a space where your heart feels completely safe to share its deepest longings, fears, truths, and vulnerabilities without any fear of judgment or criticism. If your heart could speak freely to someone you trust implicitly, what would it say? Allow your pen to flow freely across the page, capturing whatever thoughts, feelings, or desires emerge without censorship or editing. This can be a powerful way to access and acknowledge emotions that may be hidden beneath the surface of your conscious awareness, offering a pathway to deeper self-understanding and emotional release.

Engaging with these reflection questions and the journal prompt is an act of self-care and a significant step towards greater self-understanding. By taking the time to honestly explore these areas of our inner world, we can cultivate greater awareness, build stronger connections with ourselves and others, and ultimately, navigate life with more clarity, resilience, and compassion for ourselves.

Chapter 5:

Embracing

Forgiveness

The Unexpected Path to Freedom

Forgiveness after divorce can initially feel like an insurmountable task, a concept so foreign and detached from the immediate reality of heartbreak and betrayal that it might as well be written in a different language. Imagine standing at the base of a towering, jagged mountain, stripped of any climbing gear and without even the faintest outline of a trail. The summit, representing forgiveness, seems impossibly distant, shrouded in a fog of pain and resentment. In the raw aftermath of a divorce, when the wounds are still open and bleeding, the mere suggestion of forgiveness can feel like a cruel joke, an insensitive dismissal of the profound hurt you're experiencing.

"After what they did?" The thought might surge through you like a jolt of electricity, laced with disbelief and anger. "After the lies, the broken promises, the pain they inflicted? Never." This visceral reaction is entirely valid. Your feelings are real, and the hurt is undeniable. It's important to honor that pain and allow yourself the time and space to process it without the added pressure of immediate forgiveness.

But here's a truth that, while perhaps difficult to grasp in the early days, holds the key to your future freedom: Forgiveness is not about them. It's about you. This chapter isn't a decree handed down to demand that you extend forgiveness before your heart is ready. It won't offer simplistic platitudes like "just let it go," as if the pain were a switch, you could simply flick off. Nor will it minimize the significance of what happened or ask you to pretend the hurt never existed.

Instead, this chapter serves as a gentle invitation, an opportunity to tentatively explore what forgiveness could potentially mean for your own healing journey when and if you consciously choose to embrace it. It's about understanding that holding onto resentment, while a natural initial response, can ultimately become a heavy burden that you carry long after the divorce is finalized.

Because when we delve into the topic of forgiveness after divorce, we're not talking about condoning or excusing hurtful behavior. We are not suggesting that what happened was right or that the pain you endured was insignificant. Rather, we're talking about the profound act of releasing the tenacious grip that resentment has on your heart, your peace of mind, and, ultimately, your future. It's about untangling yourself from the emotional knots of anger and bitterness that can keep you tethered to the past, preventing you from fully stepping into the new chapter of your life. This unexpected path to freedom begins not with condoning the actions of another but with a profound act of self-compassion and a desire to reclaim your own inner landscape.

What Forgiveness Is (And What It's Not)

Understanding forgiveness is crucial, especially when navigating the complex emotions following a divorce. Often, our initial perceptions of forgiveness are clouded by misconceptions that can make the idea feel unappealing or even impossible. Let's dismantle some common myths and clarify what forgiveness truly entails in this context.

Common Myths About Forgiveness

1. **"Forgiving means what happened was okay."** This is perhaps the most significant misconception. Many believe that to forgive is to condone the hurtful behavior or minimize the pain caused.

2. **Truth: Forgiveness doesn't erase the past; it refuses to let the past control your future.** Forgiveness is not about saying what happened was acceptable or just. It's about acknowledging the reality of the past while consciously choosing not to let it dictate your present and future. Think of it like releasing a heavy weight you've been carrying. The weight existed; it was real, but you are choosing to put it down to ease your own burden.

3. **"I have to forgive right away."** This myth creates unnecessary pressure and can lead to feelings of guilt or failure if forgiveness doesn't come easily.

4. **Truth: Forgiveness is a process, not a deadline.** There is no set timeline for forgiveness. It unfolds at its own pace, unique to each individual and their circumstances. Allow yourself the time you need to process your emotions fully. Some days, forgiveness might feel closer; other days, it might seem distant. That's perfectly normal. Be patient and compassionate with yourself throughout this journey.

5. **"If I forgive, I have to let them back into my life."** This fear often prevents people from even considering forgiveness, especially if the relationship is unhealthy or abusive.

6. **Truth: Forgiveness and reconciliation are not the same. You can forgive from a distance.** Forgiveness is an internal act, a release within yourself. It doesn't require you to rebuild a

relationship with your ex-partner or even communicate with them. You can forgive someone without inviting them back into your life or condoning their presence. Forgiveness can be a silent, personal act of letting go of your own well-being.

What Forgiveness Actually Offers You

When you begin to understand what forgiveness truly is, its potential benefits become clearer:

- **Less time replaying painful memories:** Holding onto resentment often traps us in a cycle of replaying past hurts, keeping the pain fresh and consuming valuable mental energy. Forgiveness helps to break this cycle, allowing those memories to fade into the background rather than dominating your thoughts.
- **More energy for rebuilding your life:** The emotional energy spent on anger and bitterness can be exhausting. Forgiveness frees up this energy, allowing you to redirect it towards healing, personal growth, and building a fulfilling new chapter in your life.
- **Freedom from the exhausting weight of bitterness:** Bitterness is a heavy burden that can weigh you down emotionally and even physically. Forgiveness offers a pathway to release this weight, bringing a sense of lightness and peace.

Reflection: "If forgiveness were a gift, I could give myself, what might it make space for in my life?" This question encourages you to consider the positive possibilities that opening yourself to forgiveness might unlock. It shifts the focus from the past hurt to the potential for a brighter future.

What Forgiveness Actually Offers You

While the act of forgiveness might initially feel like a gift to the person who caused you pain, the truth is that its most profound benefits are reaped by you, the one who chooses to forgive, understanding these offerings can be a powerful motivator on the often-challenging path towards letting go.

One of the most significant gifts of forgiveness is less time replaying painful memories. When we hold onto resentment, we essentially keep the past alive in our minds. The hurtful events and words can loop endlessly, dominating our thoughts and preventing us from fully engaging with the present. It's like having a broken record stuck on a painful track. Forgiveness, however, begins to quiet this mental replay. It allows those memories to recede into the background, no longer holding center stage in our minds. This newfound mental space can bring a sense of calm and allow you to focus on the here and now rather than being constantly dragged back into the pain of the past.

Furthermore, forgiveness offers more energy for rebuilding your life. Holding onto anger, bitterness, and resentment is an incredibly draining endeavor. It consumes significant emotional and mental energy, leaving you feeling depleted and exhausted. This energy could be far better spent on nurturing yourself, exploring new interests, building new relationships, and creating a future that feels fulfilling and joyful. When you release the grip of resentment, you free up this vital energy, allowing you to invest in your own healing and growth. It's like shedding a heavy backpack that you didn't even realize you were carrying, suddenly feeling lighter and more capable of moving forward.

Perhaps the most profound benefit of forgiveness is the freedom from the exhausting weight of bitterness. Bitterness is a corrosive emotion that can seep into every aspect of your life, affecting your mood, your outlook, and even your physical health. It can create a lens of negativity through which you view the world and your interactions with others. Forgiveness acts as an antidote to this poison. By choosing to let go of bitterness, you liberate yourself from its heavy burden. This newfound lightness can bring a sense of peace, joy, and renewed hope, allowing you to move forward with a more positive and open heart.

Finally, the Reflection: "If forgiveness were a gift, I could give myself, what might it make space for in my life?" This question is designed to help you visualize the positive impact that forgiveness could have on your life. It encourages you to think beyond the pain and consider the possibilities that might emerge when you release resentment. What new emotions, experiences, or relationships might flourish in the space that bitterness once occupied? This personal reflection can be a powerful motivator, connecting you to the tangible rewards that forgiveness can offer.

The Stages of Forgiveness (It's Okay to Start Small)

Forgiveness isn't a sudden epiphany or a magical switch that flips from resentment to peace. It's a gradual, unfolding journey with its own unique rhythm and terrain.

It's perfectly alright to take small steps, to linger in certain phases, and even to backtrack at times. Be patient with yourself and trust the process.

1. The Anger Phase: "I have every right to be furious."

This initial phase is often characterized by intense anger, frustration, and a deep sense of injustice. You've likely been hurt, betrayed, or deeply disappointed, and feeling angry is a natural and valid response. Don't try to suppress it or tell yourself you shouldn't feel this way.

What helps: Allow yourself healthy outlets for this rage. Scream into a pillow to release the pent-up frustration without harming yourself or others. Write a brutally honest letter detailing every grievance, every hurt, every angry thought – then, importantly, destroy it. This allows you to express your anger fully without the need to send it or dwell on the potential consequences. Let yourself feel the heat of the rage without judgment. Acknowledge its presence and allow it to exist without letting it consume you entirely. This phase is about validating your pain and the natural anger that arises from it.

2. The Grief Phase: "How could someone I loved do this?"

As the initial intensity of anger begins to subside, it often gives way to grief. This phase involves acknowledging the loss – not just the loss of the marriage but also the loss of the dreams you shared, the future you envisioned, and the person you thought your partner was. There might be profound sadness, confusion, and a sense of disbelief.

What helps: Allow yourself to cry. Tears are a natural and healthy way to release emotional pain. Talk to a safe person – a trusted friend, family member, or therapist – who can offer a listening ear and validation without judgment. Acknowledge that the loss is real, even if the relationship needs to end. It's okay to mourn the ending of this chapter of your life and the hopes that went with it. This phase is about acknowledging the depth of your sorrow and allowing yourself to feel the sadness that accompanies loss.

3. The Curiosity Phase: "What if I tried to see this differently?"

This phase marks a subtle shift in perspective. It's not about excusing the behavior but rather about beginning to explore the experience with a touch of intellectual and emotional distance. You might start asking questions not to assign blame but to understand.

What helps: Ask yourself: "What if I tried to see this differently?" This encourages you to step outside your immediate emotional reaction and consider alternative viewpoints, even if they are uncomfortable. Also, ask: "What did this experience teach me about my boundaries?" This can help you identify areas where your boundaries might have been crossed or where you need to establish clearer boundaries in future relationships. Finally, consider: "What did this experience teach me about my strength?" Divorce, while painful, often reveals an inner resilience you might not have known you possessed. This phase is about seeking understanding and identifying the lessons learned from the experience.

4. The Release Phase: "I don't want to carry this anymore."

This phase is characterized by a growing desire to let go of the pain and resentment. It's a conscious decision to no longer allow the past to dictate your present. This doesn't necessarily mean you forget what happened, but rather that you choose not to be defined by it.

What helps: Engage in rituals like burning a symbolic item that represents the pain or the relationship. This can be a tangible way to signify your intention to let go. You can also simply whisper to yourself: "I let go for me." This is a powerful affirmation that centers the act of release on your own well-being. This phase is about actively choosing to release the emotional burden you've been carrying.

Note: These phases aren't linear. You might find yourself looping back to anger or grief even after experiencing curiosity or release. That's perfectly normal. Forgiveness is a complex process with its own ebb and flow. Be patient and kind to yourself as you navigate these stages. Remember, starting small is perfectly acceptable. Even a tiny step towards release is progress.

Forgiving Yourself (The Most Overlooked Step)

In the aftermath of a divorce, our focus naturally gravitates towards the actions of our former partners and the pain they may have caused. We analyze, we ruminate, and we often grapple with the immense task of forgiving them. However, there's a crucial aspect of healing that is frequently overlooked yet profoundly impactful: forgiving yourself. Often, the harshest critic we face in the mirror is ourselves, and the burden of self-blame can be heavier than any resentment we harbor towards our ex.

It's easy to fall into Common Self-Blame Traps after a marriage ends. The human mind often seeks explanations and can latch onto feelings of personal responsibility, even when the situation is complex and multifaceted.

"I should have seen the signs." This is a common refrain fueled by hindsight bias. It's easy to look back and identify red flags that might seem obvious now. However, during the relationship, emotions, hopes, and a desire to make things work often cloud our judgment. Be kind to yourself; you acted with the information and emotional capacity you had at the time. You weren't intentionally ignoring signs; you were likely navigating a complex emotional landscape.

"I failed at marriage." The societal pressure to have a successful marriage can lead to deep feelings of failure when it ends. However, marriage is a partnership, and its success or failure rarely rests solely on one person. External factors, incompatibility, and the choices of both individuals contribute to the outcome. Reframe this thought: the marriage ended, but that doesn't equate to personal failure. It signifies the end of one chapter and the beginning of another.

"I'll never trust myself again." The pain of a failed relationship can erode self-trust, leading to fear of making future mistakes in judgment. However, every experience, even painful ones, provides valuable lessons. Instead of viewing the past as a testament to your inability to trust yourself, see it as an opportunity to learn more about your needs, boundaries, and what you seek in future relationships.

How to Begin Self-Forgiveness is a gentle process that requires patience and compassion.

Start by learning to talk to your past self like a friend. Imagine your younger self going through this difficult time. What would you say to them? You would likely offer comfort, understanding, and reassurance. Extend that same kindness to yourself now. Remember, "You did the best you could with what you knew then." Acknowledge your efforts, your intentions, and the limitations of your knowledge and experience at that time.

Next, list what you've learned. Every experience, even painful ones, offers valuable lessons. Reflect on what the divorce has taught you about yourself, your needs, your boundaries, and what you desire in future connections. For example, you might realize, "I now know my worth isn't tied to making a relationship work," or "I understand the importance of clear communication." Focusing on the growth you've experienced can help shift the narrative from failure to learning.

Finally, make amends with yourself. This doesn't necessarily involve grand gestures but rather small, intentional acts of self-compassion and a commitment to moving forward differently. Try a simple affirmation like, "Next time, I'll listen to my instincts sooner," or "I will prioritize my own well-being." These small promises to yourself can help rebuild self-trust and foster a sense of agency.

Take the time for the Exercise: Write a letter to your younger self. Imagine the version of you who was going through the initial stages of the divorce. What words of comfort, validation, and hope do they need to hear? What wisdom have you gained that you can share with them? This act of writing can be incredibly therapeutic, allowing you to offer yourself the compassion and understanding you truly deserve.

Forgiving yourself is not about excusing past mistakes but about releasing the burden of self-blame and allowing yourself to move forward with grace and self-acceptance. It's a crucial step in reclaiming your peace and building a brighter future. Be patient and kind to yourself throughout this often-overlooked yet essential part of the healing process.

When Forgiveness Feels Out of Reach

It's important to acknowledge that forgiveness isn't always a straightforward process. Some wounds inflicted during a divorce can run so deep that the idea of complete forgiveness feels utterly impossible, a distant and unattainable ideal. In these situations, it's crucial to be gentle with yourself and recognize that healing can take many forms. If you find yourself stuck and forgiveness feels like an insurmountable mountain, there are alternative approaches that can still lead to a sense of peace and freedom.

Consider the concept of "Good Enough Forgiveness." This acknowledges that complete and total forgiveness might not always be achievable or even necessary for healing. Instead, it focuses on finding a way to move forward without being consumed by resentment. Here are a few examples of what "Good Enough Forgiveness" might look like:

"I don't forgive what they did, but I'm working to not let it define me." This approach centers on reclaiming your personal power. It acknowledges the hurt and injustice you experienced without demanding that you excuse the behavior. The focus shifts to preventing the past from dictating your present and future. It's about refusing to allow your ex-partner's actions to continue to have a negative impact on your life, even if you haven't fully forgiven them.

"I forgive the person, not the actions." This involves separating the individual from their behavior. You might not be able to forgive the specific hurtful actions, but you can acknowledge the person's humanity (however flawed) and choose to release the intense emotional attachment to the anger those actions caused. This can create a sense of distance and allow you to move forward without the constant weight of the specific incidents.

"Today, I'll let go of one small piece of this anger." Forgiveness doesn't have to be an all-or-nothing endeavor. You can approach it incrementally, choosing to release a small fraction of your resentment each day or each week. This gradual process can feel more manageable and can still lead to a significant reduction in the emotional burden over time.

It's also vital to recognize When Professional Help Makes Sense. If resentment is consistently keeping you from sleeping, dominating your thoughts, or poisoning new relationships, it's a clear indication that these feelings are significantly impacting your well-being. In such cases, seeking guidance from a therapist can help you unpack these complex emotions, explore the roots of your resentment, and develop healthy coping mechanisms, even if complete forgiveness remains elusive. A therapist can provide a safe and supportive space to process your pain and help you find a path towards healing that feels authentic to you. Remember, the goal is to find a way to move forward and create a fulfilling life, even if that path doesn't perfectly align with traditional notions of forgiveness.

The Ripple Effects of Forgiveness

The decision to embrace forgiveness, even in its "good enough" form, doesn't just impact your emotional state in isolation. It sends out positive ripples that can touch various aspects of your life, leading to a more holistic sense of healing and well-being. Let's explore some of these profound effects.

On a physical level, the impact of forgiveness can be significant. Holding onto resentment and anger creates a state of chronic stress within the body. This can manifest in various physical ailments, including difficulty sleeping, headaches, digestive issues, and even a weakened immune system. By loosening resentment's grip, you allow your body to relax and release this tension. This can lead to less stress, resulting in improved sleep patterns, reduced physical discomfort, and an overall feeling of greater physical well-being. It's as if you're unburdening your physical body from an invisible weight.

The emotional benefits of forgiveness are perhaps the most immediately noticeable. When you release the heavy emotions of anger, bitterness, and resentment, you create more room for joy, peace, and contentment to enter your life. It's like decluttering your emotional landscape, making space for positive feelings to flourish. Forgiveness doesn't mean you forget the pain, but it means you no longer allow it to dominate your emotional landscape. You gain a greater sense of inner calm and are less likely to be triggered by reminders of the past.

The ripples of forgiveness also extend to your relational life. Holding onto past hurts can create walls and prevent you from forming healthy and trusting connections in the future. You might find yourself projecting past experiences onto new people or being overly guarded. By releasing the resentment from your previous relationship, you free yourself to approach new connections with an open heart and a greater capacity for trust and intimacy. This leads to the potential for healthier future connections, unburdened by the baggage of the past.

Consider the Story: "After years of bitterness, I realized My ex wasn't paying rent in my mind anymore. That space became mine again." This powerful analogy beautifully illustrates the emotional freedom that forgiveness can bring. When you hold onto resentment, your ex-partner, in a way, continues to occupy space in your thoughts and emotions, often without your conscious permission. This mental real estate is valuable and could be used for your own growth, happiness, and peace. Forgiveness is like evicting them from this space, reclaiming your mental and emotional territory, and allowing you to invest that energy in yourself and your future. It signifies a profound shift in power, where you are no longer allowing the past to dictate your present.

Closing: Forgiveness as an Act of Self-Love

Ultimately, the journey of forgiveness, especially after the pain of divorce, is not about condoning the actions of another or letting them off the hook. At its core, forgiveness is an act of profound self-love. It's a conscious choice you make to release yourself from the shackles of resentment and bitterness, allowing your own heart to heal and your spirit to soar.

Remember, forgiveness isn't a mountain you summit all at once. It's a path you walk step by step; some days, you move forward, and other days, pause to rest.There will be moments of clarity and progress, and there might be times when old hurts resurface. This is a natural part of the process. Be gentle with yourself and honor where you are on that path today. There is no right or wrong pace, only your own.

Every time you choose to release a bit of anger, every time you offer yourself compassion for the pain you've endured, you are actively nurturing your own well-being. Because every time you choose peace over punishment, for them or yourself, you reclaim a little more of your light. That light represents your inner joy, your resilience, and your capacity for a fulfilling future. By letting go of the darkness of resentment, you allow your own inner light to shine brighter, illuminating your path forward.

This journey of self-love through forgiveness is a testament to your strength and your commitment to your own healing. Embrace the process, be patient with yourself, and know that each step you take, no matter how small, is an act of kindness towards yourself and a powerful move towards a more peaceful and joyful future. You deserve to be free from the burden of the past, and forgiveness is the key that unlocks that freedom.

Reflection Questions: A Path to Self-Understanding

Engaging in thoughtful reflection is a powerful way to navigate the complex terrain of forgiveness and ultimately find a path towards inner peace. These questions are designed to gently guide your introspection and encourage you to explore your feelings and beliefs about letting go of resentment. Take some time to truly consider each one, allowing your honest responses to surface without judgment.

What's one small grudge I'm ready to release? (Even just 5%?) The journey of forgiveness can feel overwhelming, especially when dealing with significant hurt. This question encourages you to start small, to identify a minor grievance, a lingering annoyance, or a tiny sliver of resentment that you might be willing to let go of, even if it feels like just a fraction of the whole. Think about a situation or a person where you hold a small amount of negativity. Releasing even this seemingly insignificant weight can create a surprising sense of lightness and build valuable momentum for tackling larger, more deeply rooted hurts. It's about taking that first manageable step on the path towards greater inner peace, proving to yourself that letting go is possible. Aha moment: Recognizing that even a small act of release can create a noticeable shift in your emotional burden and pave the way for further forgiveness.

How has holding onto resentment cost me? This question invites you to consider the personal toll that bitterness and anger have taken on your life. Think beyond the immediate emotional pain you feel when you dwell on the past. Has holding onto resentment affected your sleep patterns, leaving you feeling drained and unrested? Has it strained your relationships with others, perhaps making you more guarded or reactive? Has it negatively impacted your overall outlook on life, coloring your perspective with cynicism or negativity? Has it consumed your precious thoughts and energy, preventing you from fully engaging in the present moment and embracing new possibilities? Identifying the specific ways in which holding onto resentment has cost, you can provide a powerful and personal motivation to actively explore the possibility of forgiveness as you begin to recognize what you stand to gain by letting go of this heavy burden. Aha moment: Gaining a clearer understanding of the tangible and intangible costs of your resentment can provide a strong impetus for embracing forgiveness as a path to personal freedom.

If forgiveness were a color, what would it look like? (Try drawing it.) This question gently taps into your intuitive and creative side, moving beyond purely logical or verbal processing to access your deeper feelings about forgiveness. Consider the emotions and sensations you associate with forgiveness – perhaps a sense of peace, a feeling of release, a glimmer of hope, or a feeling of lightness. What color immediately embodies these feelings for you? Is it a soft, calming hue like gentle blue or serene green? Or perhaps a more vibrant, energetic shade like warm yellow or hopeful gold? There are absolutely no right or wrong answers here. Allow yourself to simply notice what color comes to mind. The act of visualizing or even taking the time to draw this color without overthinking it can offer a deeper, more visceral understanding of what forgiveness might represent for you on a personal level and can sometimes unlock emotions or insights that words alone might fail to fully capture. Aha moment: Connecting with a visual representation of forgiveness can offer a more profound and personal understanding of its meaning and potential impact on your well-being.

.

Chapter 6:

The Dawn of a New Day

The Whispers of a New Beginning

There will come a time, perhaps when you least expect it, when a subtle shift occurs within you. It might arrive with the quiet stillness of a new morning. You might awaken and sense that the heaviness you've been carrying has subtly altered, the weight on your chest feeling just a fraction lighter. The intense heat of anger that once consumed you might have softened, now glowing with the gentler warmth of fading embers. As you inhale deeply, you might notice, with a quiet surprise, that your breath flows freely, no longer catching on the sharp edges of sorrow.

This moment, however small it may seem, is significant. It is the first light breaking through the clouds after a long and difficult storm. This is the dawn of your new day, a gentle unveiling of the possibilities that lie ahead.

This newfound lightness might feel delicate, almost fragile. You might approach it with a sense of caution, perhaps even a touch of disbelief as if waiting for the familiar weight to return. It's understandable to feel this way after navigating such a significant life change. But please know that this moment is real, and it belongs entirely to you. You have journeyed through a challenging period weathered the darkness of divorce, and now, you are beginning to glimpse what lies beyond. A life that is still uniquely yours to shape, still filled with opportunities for connection and joy, and most importantly, still yours to love.

This chapter isn't here to pretend that the storm you weathered never happened. Your experiences are valid, and the pain you endured is real. Instead, this is an invitation to learn how to stand in the sunlight once more. Not as the person you were before the storm, but as someone who has emerged with a deeper understanding of yourself, a newfound inner strength, and a tenderness towards your own heart that you might not have known was possible. We will explore this new terrain together, recognizing the growth that has occurred and embracing the potential of this fresh start. Know that you are not alone in this journey towards the dawn of your new day.

Noticing the Gentle Signs of Progress

The journey of healing after a significant life change like divorce isn't always marked by grand pronouncements or dramatic breakthroughs. More often, it unfolds in a series of quiet, almost imperceptible moments. These might seem like small occurrences on their own, but when you begin to notice them, they serve as gentle whispers, assuring you that you are indeed moving forward and that a new chapter is beginning to dawn within you.

Think about it: have you recently found yourself experiencing these subtle shifts?

- **You laughed today, really laughed, and didn't feel guilty about it.** Perhaps a silly joke from a friend, a funny scene in a movie, or even just an unexpected moment of absurdity in your day brought forth a genuine, unburdened laugh. Notice if that laughter wasn't immediately followed by a pang of guilt or a fleeting thought of whether you "should" be feeling happy. This ability to experience pure joy without the shadow of the past is a powerful indicator that you are freeing yourself from its hold.

- **A memory of your ex surfaced, and instead of pain, you felt... nothing. Just a passing thought.** Perhaps a familiar place, a song on the radio, or a shared acquaintance brought your former partner to mind. But this time, the sharp pang of heartache, the wave of anger, or the familiar sting of sadness didn't follow. Instead, it was simply a neutral observation, a fleeting acknowledgment of a past that no longer holds the same emotional charge. This signifies a significant step towards emotional detachment and a reclaiming of your inner peace.

- **You made a decision for yourself without hearing their voice in your head.** Perhaps it was a simple choice about how to spend your evening, what to eat for dinner, or how to approach a work project. Did you find yourself making that decision based on your own genuine desires and needs without the internal dialogue or consideration of your former partner's opinions or preferences? This newfound autonomy in your decision-making is a clear indication that you are reconnecting with your own inner compass and forging your own path forward.

Please understand that these are not small things. They are not insignificant moments to be brushed aside. Instead, they are tangible proof that the ground beneath you is steadying. They are quiet confirmations that the healing process is underway, even if it doesn't always feel like a dramatic transformation. Pay attention to these gentle shifts within yourself. Notice these moments of unburdened joy, neutral recollection, and independent thought. They are the subtle signs that the dawn of your new chapter has indeed begun, and with each passing day, that light will continue to grow stronger. Be kind to yourself, acknowledge your progress, and trust in your own resilience. You are doing far better than you might realize.

Reclaiming Your Identity: Discovering Who You Are Now

The ending of a marriage is not just the dissolution of a partnership; it can also feel like the unraveling of the identity you carefully wove together within that relationship. Roles you played, expectations you held, and even parts of your personality might have become intertwined with your life as a couple. When that structure dissolves, it's natural to feel a sense of uncertainty, a question mark hanging over "Who am I now?"

But within this space of uncertainty lies a powerful opportunity – a chance to rediscover the core of who you are, unburdened by the expectations and dynamics of the past. This is a time to gently peel back the layers and reconnect with the individual you are, independent and whole.

Consider these questions as you embark on this journey of self-discovery:

- **What parts of myself did I set aside during my marriage?** Think back to your interests, passions, and hobbies before or even during your marriage. Were there things you enjoyed doing, skills you loved to use, or aspects of your personality that took a backseat to the needs or preferences of the relationship? This is a wonderful time to revisit those parts of yourself, to dust them off and see if they still resonate. Perhaps you once loved to paint, play a musical instrument, or spend hours lost in a good book. Now is your chance to welcome those forgotten joys back into your life.

- **What do I actually like, not what I was expected to like?** Over time, we can sometimes adopt the preferences or interests of our partners or feel pressure to conform to certain expectations within the relationship. Now, with that dynamic shifted, you have the freedom to explore what truly brings you joy and fulfillment without any external pressures. What kind of music do *you* genuinely enjoy? What types of activities make *you* feel energized and alive? What kind of food do *you* truly crave? This is an exploration of your authentic self, free from the "shoulds" and "oughts" of the past.

- **How do I want to spend my time when it's entirely my own?** This is an invitation to envision a life designed by you, for you. How do you want to fill your days and evenings? What kind of routines and rituals would nurture your well-being? Do you crave solitude and quiet reflection, or do you feel energized by social interaction? This is your opportunity to intentionally create a life that aligns with your values and desires without needing to compromise or accommodate another's schedule or preferences.

Try This: Dedicate some time, even if it's just an hour, to doing something purely because it delights you. No need for explanations, no apologies necessary. Perhaps it's taking a long bath, going for a solo hike, visiting a museum, or simply indulging in your favorite treat. This simple act can be a powerful reminder of your own capacity for joy and self-nurturing.

Remember, reclaiming your identity is a gentle process of exploration and self-compassion. There's no rush to have all the answers right away. Be patient with yourself, allow yourself to evolve, and embrace the journey of discovering who you are now in this new and exciting chapter of your life. This is your time to shine as the unique and wonderful individual you are.

The Art of Starting Over: Honoring Your Own Rhythm

There's often an unspoken narrative in our society that after a significant life event like divorce, there should be a dramatic "glow up" – a swift and flawless transformation into a seemingly perfect, thriving individual. While it's wonderful to witness and experience positive growth, it's crucial to understand that healing isn't about performance. There's no need to rush or to feel pressured to fit into someone else's idea of what your fresh start should look like. This is your journey, and it unfolds at its own unique pace.

The most important aspect of starting over is giving yourself permission:

- **To have days where you still feel wobbly.** Healing is not a linear progression. There will be days when you feel strong and empowered, ready to embrace the future. And then there will be other days when the weight of the past feels heavier, and you might feel a little unsteady. This is perfectly normal. Allow yourself these moments of vulnerability without judgment. It's a sign that you are processing and integrating your experiences.

- **To change your mind about what you want.** As you navigate this new chapter, your desires, goals, and even your sense of self might evolve. What felt right in the immediate aftermath of your divorce might shift as you gain more clarity and understanding. Give yourself the freedom to change your mind, explore different paths, and redefine what happiness and fulfillment look like for you now. There are no rules saying you have to stick to a particular vision if it no longer resonates.
- **To rebuild at your own pace.** There is no timeline for healing or for creating a new life. Comparing your journey to others or feeling pressured to "move on" quickly can be detrimental to your well-being. Honor your own rhythm. Some may find solace in diving into new experiences right away, while others may need more time for quiet reflection and gradual steps forward. Both are valid. Trust your inner guidance and move at a pace that feels comfortable and authentic for you.

Here are some Ways to Honor Your Fresh Start in your own time and in your own way:

- **Symbolic gestures:** These can be powerful ways to mark the beginning of a new chapter. Consider **donating old wedding photos** or items that hold painful memories. **Rearranging furniture** in your home can create a fresh perspective and a sense of new beginnings. **Planting something new**, whether it's a flower, a tree, or even a small herb garden, can symbolize growth and the promise of the future. These tangible actions can help to solidify your intention to move forward.

- **Small rebellions:** These are acts of reclaiming your personal freedom and rediscovering what brings you joy without the constraints of the past. Maybe it's finally **eating dessert for dinner** just because you want to, **staying up late** to watch a movie without anyone else's schedule to consider, or **wearing that outfit you were once told was "too much."** These small acts of self-indulgence and self-expression can be incredibly liberating.
- **Quiet affirmations:** These are gentle reminders you give yourself to reinforce your worthiness and your right to happiness. Repeating affirmations like **"I am allowed to take up space," "I am allowed to be happy,"** or **"I am worthy of love and joy"** can help to build self-esteem and cultivate a more positive inner dialogue as you navigate this new phase.

Remember, starting over is not about erasing the past but about creating a future that feels authentic and fulfilling for you without the added weight of societal pressure or unrealistic expectations. Be kind to yourself, celebrate your progress, no matter how small, and trust in your ability to build a beautiful new life at your own pace.

Navigating the World as a "Single" You

Re-entering the social landscape after divorce can sometimes feel like stepping into unfamiliar territory. For so long, you may have navigated the world as part of a "we," and now, transitioning to a "single" you within existing social circles can bring about a mix of emotions and uncertainties. It's natural to feel a little like the odd piece in a puzzle, wondering where you fit and how you navigate interactions that were once defined by your couple's status.

You might find yourself pondering questions like:

- **How do I introduce myself now?** This can feel surprisingly awkward. Do you simply state your name? Do you mention your divorce? Do you feel the need to explain? Remember, you have the agency to decide how much you share. A simple "Hi, I'm [Your Name]" is perfectly sufficient. If the conversation evolves, you can share more if and when you feel comfortable. There's no need to lead with your marital status unless you choose to.

- **Will people see me differently?** It's understandable to wonder if your social standing or how others perceive you will change. Some friends might not know how to react, while others might have their own assumptions or biases. Try to focus on the genuine connections you have and remember that true friends will value you for who you are, regardless of your relationship status. If some perceptions do shift, that might simply reveal who your authentic supporters truly are.

- **Do I even fit in anywhere anymore?** This feeling of displacement is common. You might find that social gatherings that once felt natural now feel a little off-kilter. It's okay if you need some time to adjust or if you discover that some social dynamics have shifted. This can also be an opportunity to explore new social circles and find connections that resonate with who you are becoming now.

Here are some Gentle Reminders for Social Reentry:

- **You don't owe anyone an explanation for your single status.** While some people might be curious, you are not obligated to share the details of your divorce with everyone you encounter. You can offer a brief and simple response if asked or politely decline to discuss it further if you prefer. Your personal life is yours to share on your own terms.

- **It's okay to decline events that feel overwhelming.** Socializing can be emotionally taxing, especially in the early stages of navigating life as a single person. If an invitation feels like more than you can handle, it is perfectly acceptable to politely decline. Prioritize your well-being and engage in social activities when you feel ready and comfortable.

- **New connections await, ones that align with who you're becoming.** While it might feel like your existing social world has shifted, remember that this is also an opportunity to forge new connections with people who share your current interests and values. Be open to meeting new people through hobbies, activities, or mutual acquaintances. These new relationships can be incredibly supportive and affirming as you build your new life.

Here's a simple Script for Awkward Moments:

Scenario	Possible Response
Being asked about your ex at a social gathering	"We're no longer together, but I'm doing well." or "I'm focusing on new things."
Feeling pressured to bring a plus-one	"I'm enjoying connecting with everyone on my own tonight, thank you."
Friends making assumptions about your availability.	"I appreciate the invite! Let me check my schedule and get back to you."

Remember to be patient and kind to yourself as you navigate this aspect of your new chapter. Finding your footing in the social world as a single person takes time and adjustment. Trust that you will find your place and build connections that nurture and support the wonderful person you are becoming.

The Gift of Looking Forward: Gently Turning Towards Tomorrow

For a significant period after your divorce, it's understandable that your thoughts and energy might have been heavily focused on the past. Processing what happened, understanding the "whys," and navigating the emotional fallout are all vital parts of the healing journey. But there will come a time when you might notice a subtle yet significant shift – a gentle stirring of curiosity about what lies ahead. This is a precious gift, a sign that you are beginning to release the heavy anchor of the past and tentatively turn your gaze towards the horizon of your future.

This newfound sense of looking forward might feel unfamiliar, perhaps even a little strange at first. After being so consumed by the events of the past, allowing yourself to dream and envision possibilities might seem daunting. But embrace this feeling; it's a beautiful indicator of your resilience and your innate desire for growth and happiness.

Here are some gentle ways to begin Dreaming Again (Start Small):

- **List three places you'd like to visit, even if just a new café in town.** This exercise isn't about planning an elaborate vacation right away. It's about allowing yourself to think about new experiences and possibilities, no matter how small. Perhaps there's a local bookstore you've been meaning to explore, a park in a neighboring town, or even a far-off destination that sparks your interest. Simply jotting these down can open up a sense of anticipation and remind you that there's still so much of the world to experience.
- **Imagine your ideal day a year from now. What's different?** Take a few quiet moments to envision what a positive and fulfilling day might look like for you in the future. What are you doing? Who are you spending time with? How do you feel? This isn't about setting rigid expectations but rather about allowing yourself to cultivate a hopeful vision for your life and identify areas where you'd like to see positive changes.
- **What's one tiny risk you're ready to take? (Example: Joining a class, texting an old friend.)** Stepping outside your comfort zone, even

in small ways, can be incredibly empowering. Think about something you've been considering but perhaps felt hesitant to do. It could be joining a pottery class, reaching out to an old friend you've lost touch with, or trying a new recipe. Taking these small risks can build confidence and open doors to new experiences and connections.

It's important to remember the note provided: It's normal if this feels scary. Excitement and fear often travel together. The prospect of the unknown can naturally bring about some apprehension, even as you feel a sense of excitement about the possibilities. Acknowledge both of these feelings and be kind to yourself as you navigate them.

Here's a table that illustrates the gentle shift in focus:

Focus Area	Before (Potentially)	Now (Emerging)
Time Perspective	Dwelling on the past	Tentatively looking to the future
Emotional Core	Hurt, anger, sadness	Curiosity, hope, anticipation
Energy Direction	Analyzing what went wrong	Envisioning what could be
Action Tendency	Replaying old scenarios	Exploring new possibilities

Embracing the gift of looking forward is about giving yourself permission to dream again, to envision a future that is uniquely yours to create. It's a testament to your resilience and your unwavering capacity for hope. Allow yourself this gentle shift in perspective and trust in the exciting possibilities that lie ahead.

Closing: Your Life Is Still Yours

As the sun has risen on this new chapter, casting its gentle light on the path ahead, please know that there are no demands for immediate perfection or grand transformations. This dawn doesn't require you to suddenly become someone entirely different. It simply asks that you show up in whatever way feels authentic to you at this moment.

You might still be navigating waves of emotion, still piecing together the fragments of your heart, and that is perfectly okay. There is no need to rush the process or to feel pressured to present a flawless version of yourself to the world. This new beginning is about honoring where you are right now, with all your imperfections, your vulnerabilities, and your strength.

Remember, you are inherently worthy of every good thing that life has to offer. Your journey through divorce does not diminish your value or your right to happiness. This new chapter is an opportunity to rediscover what brings you joy, nurture your own well-being, and create a life that truly resonates with who you are now.

The dawn you are experiencing is just the beginning. It's the first glimmer of light after a long night, promising a day filled with new possibilities and experiences. There will be more sunrises to come, each bringing its own unique beauty and opportunities for growth. Be patient with yourself, allow yourself the time and space you need to heal and build and trust in your own resilience.

Your life, in all its evolving beauty, is still yours. Embrace this moment, this new beginning, with gentle hope and unwavering self-compassion. You are capable, you are worthy, and you are not alone on this journey. The dawn is just the beginning, and a whole new day awaits you.

Reflection Questions: A Path to Self-Understanding

As you stand on the threshold of this new chapter, taking a moment for thoughtful reflection can help solidify the progress you've made and intentionally plant seeds for the future you envision. These questions are gentle invitations to look both inward and forward with kindness and hope, acknowledging the journey you've traveled and the possibilities that lie ahead.

What's one thing I'm proud of overcoming? Take a moment to truly acknowledge your strength and resilience. The journey through divorce is rarely easy, and you have undoubtedly navigated a multitude of challenges and overcome numerous obstacles along the way. What is one specific hurdle you faced – perhaps a particularly difficult conversation, a moment of intense sadness you weathered, a practical challenge you successfully navigated, or a limiting belief you began to dismantle – where you felt truly tested, and yet you persevered? Recognizing your own capacity to overcome adversity, no matter how big or small the victory might seem, is incredibly empowering and serves as a potent reminder of the inner strength you possess as you continue to move forward. Every act of overcoming, every step you've taken towards healing, deserves to be acknowledged and celebrated. Aha moment: Recognizing a specific challenge you've overcome can provide a powerful boost of confidence in your ability to navigate future obstacles.

If I could tell my "just divorced" self one thing, what would it be? Imagine you have the opportunity to send a message of comfort, wisdom, and reassurance back to the version of yourself who was just beginning this often-daunting journey of divorce. What single piece of encouragement, practical advice, or profound insight would you offer? What have you learned along the way about healing, about self-care, about the importance of boundaries, or about the possibilities that the future holds that you wish your past self-had known in those early, uncertain days? This reflection can not only highlight how far you've come on your own path but also offer a profound sense of self-compassion for the pain you endured and the remarkable courage you demonstrated in those initial steps. Aha moment: Identifying the wisdom you would share with your past self can illuminate the significant growth you've experienced and offer a sense of closure and self-compassion.

What color, scent, or song feels like "new beginnings" to me? This question invites you to connect with the sensory aspects of hope and fresh starts on a deeply personal level. Is there a particular color that evokes a feeling of lightness, possibility, and optimism when you see it? Perhaps a certain scent that reminds you of a new season, a clean slate, or a feeling of renewal? Or maybe a song whose melody, lyrics, or overall feeling resonates with the sense of moving forward, of shedding the past and embracing what lies ahead? Engaging your senses in this way can create a powerful and personal anchor for the positive emotions associated with new beginnings, helping you to connect with a sense of optimism, anticipation, and the inherent hope that resides within you as you step into this new dawn of your life. Aha moment: Connecting with a specific sensory cue for "new beginnings" can create a tangible and personal source of hope and positive anticipation for the future.

Chapter 7:

Finding the Angels

The Unexpected Grace in the Broken Places

There often comes a moment in your healing journey, perhaps when you feel most overwhelmed by the weight of what has been lost when a quiet realization begins to dawn: even within this challenging experience, unexpected positive shifts can emerge. The pain of divorce can feel all-consuming, casting a shadow over every aspect of your life. Yet, if you allow yourself to look beyond the immediate hurt, you might start to recognize the subtle yet significant silver linings that can arise from this life-altering event. These are the unexpected graces, the positive outcomes that begin to illuminate the path forward.

Think of these as your "angels", not necessarily in a traditional sense, but as the positive discoveries and opportunities that can surprisingly blossom from the broken places. Perhaps, down the line, this journey will lead you to a relationship that is a far better fit for your true self and your deepest sensibilities. Maybe you'll find yourself creating a more uplifting and supportive environment in your home and life, one where you can truly thrive. For many, divorce becomes a powerful catalyst for self-discovery, an awakening to passions and aspects of themselves that were dormant or unrecognized before. You might even begin to recognize relationship patterns or red flags that were once invisible, love having perhaps clouded those obvious realizations, equipping you with invaluable wisdom for future connections.

These "angels," these silver linings, often appear when you least expect them. It might be a newfound sense of independence you didn't know you possessed, a rekindled passion for a forgotten hobby, or the realization of an inner strength you never had to call upon before. They are the positive outcomes that remind you that even within a difficult experience, growth and positive change are possible.

Aha moment: Take a moment to consider your own journey so far. Have there been any unexpected positive shifts or new understandings about yourself or your life that have emerged since your divorce? Perhaps you've discovered a newfound resilience, a clearer sense of your own needs, or a deeper appreciation for certain friendships. These are the silver linings, the "angels" in your experience.

This chapter is an invitation to open your eyes to these positive discoveries. It's not about minimizing the pain you've endured or suggesting that divorce is somehow a desirable event. Rather, it's about broadening your perspective to recognize that even amidst the difficulties, there can be unexpected gifts of growth and understanding. We will explore these potential silver linings, helping you to identify the positive outcomes that may be emerging in your life, proving that while pain is undoubtedly a part of your story, it is far from being the only chapter. By intentionally seeking out these "angels," these positive discoveries, you can begin to build a foundation of hope and strength as you navigate this new phase of your life.

The Angels Around You; Recognizing Everyday Silver Linings

It's true that in the immediate aftermath of divorce, it can feel as though the world has dimmed. However, as you begin to navigate this new terrain, you might start to notice unexpected glimmers of light in the most ordinary places. These are the "angels" we talked about – the silver linings that emerge from this significant life change, often revealing themselves through the people around you, the moments that lift you, and the wisdom you gain. They might not appear in a blaze of glory but rather in the quiet unfolding of your days.

Consider these areas where these "angels" – these positive shifts – often show up:

The People Who See You, Deeper Connections Emerge

While some relationships might shift after a divorce, you might find that others deepen in unexpected and meaningful ways. This can be a time when the authenticity of your connections truly shines through.

- **The friend who texts "How are you, really?" and means it:** This isn't just a casual greeting. It's a genuine inquiry from someone who cares deeply about your well-being and is willing to listen without judgment. Perhaps this friendship has blossomed into a more profound source of support now that you have more space to nurture it, or maybe you're seeing a new level of empathy and understanding from this person. *Aha moment: Realizing that your divorce has clarified who your true support system is, leading to deeper and more authentic friendships that truly nourish you.*

- **The coworker who covers for you on a day you just can't:** This act of kindness might feel more significant now, highlighting the supportive and understanding relationships you have in your professional life. Perhaps you've discovered a level of camaraderie and empathy from colleagues that you hadn't fully appreciated before, creating a more positive and uplifting work environment. ***Aha moment:*** *Recognizing the strength and kindness within your professional network, providing a sense of stability and support in this new phase.*

- **The support group member who nods and says, "Me too":** Finding a connection with others who understand your experience firsthand can be incredibly validating and empowering. This shared understanding can create a sense of belonging and reduce feelings of isolation, offering a unique form of support and camaraderie. ***Aha moment:*** *Discovering the power of shared experience and the comfort of knowing you're not alone in navigating this journey, leading to a sense of community and mutual support.*

Exercise: Think of one person who has been a quiet anchor for you during this time. What's one small way you can thank them (even just in your heart)? Acknowledging their support, even silently, can strengthen your appreciation for the positive connections in your life.

The Moments That Carry You – Newfound Joys and Freedoms

Divorce can unexpectedly open up space for new experiences and personal freedoms that might have been limited before. These moments can feel like little gifts that bring a sense of lightness and joy.

- **The first time you laugh so hard your stomach hurts:** This uninhibited laughter, free from any underlying tension or sadness related to your previous relationship, can feel incredibly liberating. It's a sign that you are reconnecting with your own capacity for joy and finding humor in life again. *Aha moment: Realizing the freedom to experience pure, unadulterated joy and laughter, perhaps in ways you hadn't in a while.*

- **A hot shower after a long day of holding it together:** This simple act of self-care might now feel like a luxurious and much-needed moment of peace and rejuvenation, entirely on your own terms. It's a reminder of your ability to nurture and care for yourself independently. *Aha moment: Appreciating the simple pleasures and the freedom to prioritize your own comfort and well-being.*

- **The peace of early morning before the world wakes up:** This quiet solitude might now be a cherished time for reflection, personal pursuits, or simply enjoying the stillness without the demands or expectations of a shared household. It's a newfound sense of personal space and time. *Aha moment: Recognizing the value of your own time and space and the freedom to use it in ways that truly nourish your soul.*

Practice: Keep an "Angel Journal" this week. Each day, jot down one small thing that felt like a gift – a moment of connection, a burst of joy, a moment of peaceful solitude. This practice will help you train your eyes to see these everyday silver linings.

The Wisdom That Finds You; Insights for Growth

Through the process of divorce, you inevitably gain valuable insights about yourself, relationships, and life. These moments of understanding can be powerful catalysts for personal growth.

- **A book passage that feels written just for you:** You might stumble upon words that perfectly articulate what you've been feeling or offer a new perspective on your situation, providing a sense of validation and guidance. *Aha moment: Recognizing the wisdom and guidance that can be found in unexpected places, offering clarity and understanding.*

- **A therapist's insight that unlocks something new:** Therapy can provide a safe space to process your experiences and gain valuable insights into relationship dynamics, your own patterns, and pathways to healing. *Aha moment: Gaining a deeper understanding of yourself and your past, leading to personal growth and a clearer path forward.*

- **Your own sudden realization: "I'm stronger than I thought"** You might find yourself handling challenges and navigating difficult emotions with a resilience you didn't know you possessed. This self-awareness is a powerful testament to your inner strength. *Aha moment: Recognizing your own inherent strength and resilience, empowering you to face future challenges with greater confidence.*

These "angels" – these silver linings – are all around you, often hidden in plain sight. By consciously looking for them, you begin to shift your focus towards the positive aspects that are emerging in your life, even amidst the ongoing process of healing.

The Angel Within; Your Unshakable Core

While the kindness of others and the unexpected moments of grace are invaluable, perhaps the most significant "angel," the most powerful silver lining to emerge from this journey, resides within you. It's your own unshakable core, that inner strength and resilience, that has carried you through the most challenging times. This part of you might have been tested, stretched, and perhaps even felt momentarily lost, but it has remained a constant source of inner fortitude.

Think about it. Even on the days when the weight of grief felt unbearable, something within you compelled you to keep going. Consider these powerful acts of your inner "angel":

- **Got out of bed when every bone ached with grief:** On those mornings when the mere thought of facing the day felt impossible, something deep within you found the strength to rise. This wasn't a small feat; it was an act of profound resilience, a quiet determination to keep moving forward, even when every fiber of your being longed to stay still. *Aha moment: Recognizing that even in your deepest sorrow, a powerful inner strength was at work, urging you towards the light.*
- **Chose to feed yourself even when food tasted like nothing:** When your appetite vanished, and

even the simplest tasks felt monumental, you still found a way to nourish your body. This act of self-care, even in its most basic form, was a testament to your inherent will to survive and eventually heal. It was your inner "angel", gently reminding you that you deserve to be cared for. *Aha moment: Appreciating the small acts of self-care you managed, recognizing them as powerful indicators of your inner strength and commitment to your well-being.*

- **Dared to hope again, even if just for a minute:** In the darkest moments, the idea of a brighter future might have seemed distant and impossible. Yet, even a fleeting glimmer of hope, a momentary thought of possibility, was a spark ignited by your inner "angel," a reminder that even after the storm, the sun will eventually break through the clouds. *Aha moment: Recognizing the courage it took to hold onto even the smallest sliver of hope, understanding it as a vital sign of your enduring spirit.*

How to Connect with Your Inner Angel

This inner strength, this resilient core, is always there, waiting to be acknowledged and nurtured. Here are some ways to connect with this powerful aspect of yourself:

- **Speak kindly to yourself.** The inner dialogue you have with yourself is incredibly powerful. Try consciously replacing harsh self-criticism with words of compassion and understanding. Instead of "I should have known better," try **"I did the best I could with what I knew then."** When you feel overwhelmed, remind yourself: **"You're doing the**

best you can." Treat yourself with the same gentle kindness and encouragement you would offer a dear friend going through a difficult time. ***Aha moment: Realize the profound impact of your self-talk and choose to cultivate a more compassionate and supportive inner voice.***

- **Honor your resilience.** Take a moment to reflect on the challenges you've already overcome in your life, even before this divorce. **List 3 storms you've already survived.** Perhaps it was a difficult career change, a personal loss, or another challenging relationship. Acknowledging your past resilience will remind you of your inherent ability to navigate tough times and emerge stronger. ***Aha moment: Recognizing the evidence of your past strength and building confidence in your ability to navigate this current challenge.***

- **Trust your intuition.** That quiet voice within you, that gut feeling that guides you – that's your inner wisdom speaking, your inner "angel" offering guidance. Pay attention to those subtle nudges, those intuitive hits that tell you, **"This is good for me"** or **"I need to step back."** Learning to trust your intuition is about trusting your own inner compass and recognizing your inherent wisdom. ***Aha moment: Understanding that you possess an internal guidance system that can lead you towards what is best for your healing and growth.***

- **Meditation:** Find a quiet space, place a hand gently over your heart, and take a few deep breaths. As you exhale, release any tension you might be holding. Then, whisper to yourself: **"I am still here. I am enough."** This simple practice can help you connect with the steady rhythm of your own heart, reminding you of your inherent worthiness and your enduring presence. ***Aha moment:*** *Experiencing a sense of grounding and self-acceptance through this simple act of connecting with your inner self.*

This "angel within" has been with you all along. The journey of divorce might have brought it into sharper focus, revealing the incredible strength and resilience you possess. Embrace this inner core, nurture it with kindness and self-compassion, and trust in its unwavering ability to guide you towards a brighter future. You are stronger than you think, and you are absolutely enough.

When Angels Hide; Finding Light in the Dark

There will be times on this journey, even after you've begun to recognize the subtle graces around you, when those "angels", those silver linings and moments of positive discovery, seem to retreat into the shadows. The weight of the divorce might feel heavier again, the path ahead less clear, and the light that was beginning to dawn might appear to have been temporarily extinguished. Please know, dear reader, that this ebb and flow is an inherent part of healing. Just as the sun sometimes hides behind clouds, the positive aspects might become less visible for a while. During these times, it's crucial to remember that they haven't disappeared entirely; sometimes, we simply need to adjust our focus and explore different ways of seeking them out. Be gentle with yourself during these moments, and know that it's okay to feel a little lost or disheartened. This is a natural part of processing a significant life change.

- **Look Smaller:** Focus your attention on the small, immediate comforts and graces that still exist in your present moment. It's easy to overlook these tiny glimmers when our minds are consumed by larger concerns, but they can offer significant solace. Take a moment to truly notice the warmth of your tea or coffee cup in your hands, the comforting rhythm of your own breathing, or the soft texture of a cozy blanket.

  Perhaps it's the unexpected beauty of a single flower blooming in your garden, the soothing sound of rain against the windowpane, or the familiar melody of a favorite song that brings a momentary sense of peace. Engaging your senses in this way, focusing on the here and now, can ground you and provide a gentle distraction from overwhelming emotions. *Aha moment: Even when the grander positive outcomes feel out of reach, countless small, accessible moments of comfort and simple beauty still surround you, offering tiny sparks of light in the darkness.*

- **Look Back:** When the present feels particularly challenging and the future uncertain, take a moment to intentionally reflect on the progress you've already made and the positive moments you've experienced. If you've been keeping an **"Angel Journal,"** now is a particularly valuable time to revisit those entries. Flip through the pages and remind yourself of the instances of kindness, moments of joy, and small victories you've already recorded.

Reading about this past silver linings can offer a powerful sense of hope and reassurance, reminding you that even when things feel difficult in the present, positive moments have been present in your journey and will likely appear again in the future. Beyond your journal, consider looking back at old photos, rereading supportive messages from friends, or simply reflecting on times you've felt strong and resilient. This act of looking back isn't about dwelling on the past in a negative way but rather about acknowledging your journey and reinforcing your inherent ability to find light even in challenging circumstances. ***Aha moment:*** *Gaining valuable perspective and renewed hope by consciously acknowledging the positive experiences you've already navigated on your healing journey, strengthening your belief in your own resilience and the enduring presence of goodness in your life.*

- **Be the Angel for Someone Else:** Sometimes, when our own light feels dim, shifting our focus outward and extending kindness to others can be a powerful way to rediscover the light within ourselves and in the world around us. A simple, genuine **smile at a stranger** can brighten their day, and you might be surprised by the warmth it brings back to you.

Consider **donating clothes or household items you no longer need** to a local charity; letting go of things that no longer serve you can create a sense of lightness and can also provide tangible comfort and support to someone else. Reach out to a friend who might be going through a tough time and **send a**

"No need to reply, just thinking of you" message; this simple act of care can strengthen your connections and remind you of the importance of your relationships. Perhaps you could offer to help a neighbor with a task or volunteer your time for a cause you believe in.

Helping others often has a remarkable way of revealing the "angels", the positive aspects and feelings of connection, that we might have missed in our own lives. By shifting your focus outward and becoming a source of light for someone else, you might find that your own inner light begins to rekindle. ***Aha moment:*** *Understanding that actively extending kindness, compassion, and support to others can not only bring light into their lives but also unexpectedly illuminate the positive aspects and inherent goodness within your own experience.*

Remember to be patient and gentle with yourself during these times when the "angels" seem hidden. It's okay if finding the light takes time and effort. Trust that even in the darkest moments, there are still ways to find and create light in your world. You are stronger and more resilient than you might realize, and the ability to find beauty and hope, even in the midst of challenges, is a testament to your enduring spirit.

A Life Attuned to Angels, Making It a Practice

Recognizing the "angels", those silver linings and positive discoveries, in the midst of and after divorce isn't just a one-time realization. It's a skill that can be cultivated and strengthened through conscious effort and intention. The more you actively look for these glimmers of light, the more readily you will begin to see them in your daily life. By making this awareness a regular practice, you can gently shift your focus towards the positive aspects that are emerging, fostering a greater sense of hope and resilience as you continue your healing journey.

Here are some simple yet powerful practices you can incorporate into your routine to live a life more attuned to these "angels":

- **Daily: Pause for 1 minute to name one grace (big or tiny).** Each day, take just sixty seconds to intentionally identify one thing, no matter how small it might seem, for which you feel a sense of gratitude or that felt like a positive moment in your day. It could be the warmth of the sun, a kind word from a stranger, a moment of laughter, or a sense of accomplishment. This brief pause helps to train your mind to actively seek out the good, shifting your focus away from what might be difficult. *Aha moment: Realizing the simple yet profound power of a daily gratitude practice to reframe your perspective and highlight the positive aspects that often go unnoticed.*

- **Weekly: Reach out to someone who's been an angel for you.** Think about the people who have offered you support, understanding, or kindness throughout your divorce journey. Make a conscious effort to connect with one of them each week. This could be a simple text message, a phone call, or even a brief email expressing your appreciation. Acknowledging their support not only strengthens your connection but also reinforces the positive impact they've had on your life. *Aha moment: Understanding the importance of nurturing and appreciating the supportive relationships that have emerged or deepened during this time, recognizing the invaluable role of human connection in healing.*

- **Monthly: Do something that makes you feel like an angel (e.g., volunteer, write a love letter to yourself).** Dedicate some time each month to an activity that allows you to either give back to others or nurture yourself in a deeply meaningful way. Volunteering for a cause you care about can create a sense of purpose and connection to something larger than yourself. Alternatively, writing a heartfelt letter of love and appreciation to yourself can be a powerful act of self-compassion and a reminder of your own inherent worthiness. Engaging in activities that resonate with kindness, both outward and inward, reinforces the positive energy you are cultivating. *Aha moment: Recognizing the empowering feeling that comes from both receiving and extending "angelic" acts, understanding that you have the capacity to be a source of positivity for yourself and others.*

The cumulative effect of these practices can be truly transformative. By intentionally weaving these small moments of awareness and action into your daily, weekly, and monthly routines, you begin to cultivate a mindset that is more attuned to recognizing the positive aspects of your life. This doesn't mean ignoring the challenges but rather learning to hold them alongside a growing awareness of the good that is also present. As you continue to practice seeing with these new eyes, you will likely find that the "angels", those silver linings and moments of grace, appear more frequently and more vividly, offering ongoing support and hope as you embrace this new chapter of your life.

Closing: The Miracle of Noticing

The truth is, dear reader, that the "angels", those silver linings, moments of grace, and unexpected positive discoveries, were likely present around you all along, even during the most challenging times of your divorce journey. The real miracle isn't their sudden appearance but rather the shift within you that has allowed you to finally see them. After navigating so much pain and uncertainty, your heart and mind have opened in new ways, enabling you to recognize the subtle yet significant goodness that surrounds you and resides within you.

This newfound ability to notice these "angels" changes everything. It doesn't erase the difficulties you've faced, nor does it diminish the validity of your pain. Instead, it offers a broader perspective, a gentle reminder that even in the midst of hardship, there are still glimmers of light, moments of connection, and seeds of hope to be found. This shift in perception is a powerful testament to your healing and your growing capacity to find beauty and meaning in your everyday experiences.

Think back to the beginning of this chapter. You might have felt as though the pain of divorce had drained all the light from the world. But as you've explored the "angels" around you and within you, you've hopefully begun to recognize that goodness persists, even here, even now. You've acknowledged the kindness of others, the comfort of simple moments, the wisdom gained, and the strength of your own resilient spirit. These are not fleeting illusions; they are real, and they are yours to embrace.

And this is the profound promise of learning to notice these "angels": because once you know how to look for light, you'll never again be left in total darkness. Even on the days when the shadows feel long and overwhelming, you will have the ability to seek out those small, quiet mercies, those reminders that you are not alone and that hope is always present, waiting to be found. This is a skill that will continue to develop and deepen as you move forward, allowing you to navigate future challenges with a greater sense of inner peace and resilience.

Embrace this newfound way of seeing, dear friend. Continue to practice noticing the "angels" in your life, both big and small. Trust in your own inner strength, and know that even after the storm of divorce, you are surrounded by unexpected grace and filled with an unshakeable core of resilience. The ability to see the light is a gift you have given yourself, and it will illuminate your path towards a brighter and more hopeful future.

Reflection Questions: A Path to Self-Understanding

These reflection questions are designed to gently guide you in cultivating this new way of seeing the world – a perspective that is more attuned to recognizing the "angels," those silver linings and moments of grace that often surround us, even amidst challenging times. Take a few quiet moments with these prompts, allowing your honest thoughts and feelings to surface without judgment. There are no right or wrong answers, only opportunities for deeper self-awareness and a shift in focus.

What's one angel I overlooked today? As you reflect on your day, try to gently shift your focus beyond the difficulties or frustrations you might have encountered. Were there any small, perhaps seemingly insignificant, acts of kindness you received from others or witnessed in the world around you that you might have initially dismissed or not fully appreciated? Perhaps a stranger offered a genuine smile, a friend sent an unexpected and encouraging message, a colleague offered a helping hand, or you simply noticed a fleeting moment of unexpected beauty in nature, like a vibrant sunset or a bird singing its heart out. Sometimes, these subtle moments of grace pass by without our full attention in the busyness of our day. By consciously looking back with intention, you can begin to train your eyes to recognize these everyday "angels" and cultivate a deeper appreciation for the goodness that is often present, even in seemingly ordinary moments. This practice helps to weave a tapestry of positive threads into the fabric of your daily experience. Aha moment: Recognizing the abundance of small acts of kindness and beauty you might have overlooked can shift your perspective towards a more appreciative view of the world.

When have I been an angel for myself without realizing it? This question invites you to turn that gentle and compassionate gaze inward and acknowledge your own inherent strength, resilience, and acts of self-care. Think about the ways you consciously or unconsciously cared for yourself today, even in small, seemingly insignificant ways. Did you take a moment to breathe deeply when feeling overwhelmed? Did you choose a nourishing meal or a comforting warm drink when you could have opted for something less supportive? Did you offer yourself a word of encouragement or a moment of rest when self-doubt or fatigue crept in? These acts of self-care, self-compassion, and perseverance, no matter how small they might seem, are all ways in which your own inner "angel" shows up for you, offering comfort and support. Recognizing these moments can foster a deeper sense of self-appreciation and highlight the inherent strength and kindness you possess within. Aha moment: Acknowledging your own acts of self-care and resilience as your "inner angel" at work can foster a deeper sense of self-appreciation and strength.

If my inner angel had a message for me right now, what would it be? Take a quiet moment to connect with your intuition, that gentle, unwavering inner voice of wisdom and guidance that resides within you. If that compassionate and knowing part of you – your own inner "angel" – had a message to share with you at this very moment, without any judgment or expectation, what do you sense it might be? Perhaps it's a message of reassurance, gently reminding you of your strength and resilience. Maybe it's an encouragement to be patient with yourself during this process or to embrace a particular opportunity that has presented itself. By taking a few moments of stillness to tune into this inner voice, you can tap into a deep well of wisdom and receive guidance that is uniquely tailored to your individual journey and your specific needs at this moment. Aha moment: Connecting with your intuition and receiving a personal message from your "inner angel" can provide a sense of comfort, clarity, and direction that is uniquely yours.

Chapter 8:

The Phoenix Moment

The Journey of Becoming: Identity After Divorce

The ending of a marriage is far more than the conclusion of a legal agreement or the division of shared belongings. It often acts as a profound disruption, one that can unravel the very narrative you've carefully constructed about yourself over the years. The roles you inhabited within the partnership, the definitions you embraced, can suddenly feel like they've been pulled out from under you. You might have identified strongly as "a partner," someone deeply intertwined with another's life. Perhaps you saw yourself as "part of a team," working in tandem towards shared goals and dreams. Or maybe, at your core, you believed "I was someone who could make love last," a definition that now feels challenged and uncertain.

When these deeply ingrained understandings of who you are begin to fall away, it can feel as though the foundations of your identity have shifted. What remains in their absence? Initially, this space might feel like standing in an empty room where the walls you once relied on for structure and definition have vanished without a trace. It can be disorienting, leaving you feeling unmoored and unsure of your bearings. This emptiness can even feel terrifying, as the familiar outlines of yourself seem to have blurred or disappeared entirely.

But within this very space, this seemingly desolate landscape, lies a profound and often unexpected opportunity if you allow yourself to see it with open eyes and a courageous heart, a space brimming with possibility. This chapter is dedicated to exploring that sacred and transformative period between who you were within the context of your marriage and who you will become as you step into this new chapter of your life. It's not about trying to simply "get over" your past or pretending that the shared story never existed. Instead, it's about the gentle and courageous work of gathering the scattered pieces of yourself, the experiences, the lessons, the core essence of who you are, and discovering, with tenderness and unwavering curiosity, how they might fit together in a new and perhaps even more authentic way now.

Please know, with absolute certainty, that you are not broken. You are not a collection of shattered pieces beyond repair. Rather, you are in the midst of a powerful and transformative process, the process of becoming. This is a time of profound personal evolution, an opportunity to redefine yourself on your own terms, embrace new aspects of your being, and emerge from this experience wiser, stronger, and more deeply connected to your truest self. Embrace this journey with compassion for yourself, allowing for moments of uncertainty and vulnerability while also holding onto the exciting potential that lies within this uncharted territory of self-discovery.

The Blank Canvas: Why Identity Feels Lost After Divorce

Marriage, in its beautiful complexity, often involves the weaving together of two individual lives into a shared tapestry. Over time, "you" and "your partner" can naturally blend into a "we," a collective identity defined by shared experiences, routines, and aspirations. This merging can bring immense joy and a sense of belonging, but when that partnership dissolves through divorce, it can leave behind a feeling of profound disorientation, as if a significant part of who you were has also vanished. This is why the canvas of your identity might feel blank, waiting to be redefined.

Think about how deeply intertwined your lives might have become. So many aspects of your daily existence likely involve your partner, from the mundane to the deeply personal. In the separation, you might find yourself:

- **Struggling to make decisions without automatically considering your ex's preferences.** Perhaps you always consulted them on everything from what to watch on television to larger life choices like career moves or home decor. Now, facing decisions independently can feel strange and even daunting, as if a familiar sounding board is missing. You might find yourself pausing, almost expecting their input, before realizing you now have the freedom – and perhaps the challenge – of choosing for yourself.
- **Feeling strange doing activities you once shared.** Whether it was a regular Sunday morning brunch, a favorite hiking trail, or even just watching a particular television show together, engaging in these activities, solo can feel unsettling. These shared moments were part of the fabric of your "we," and doing them alone can bring up feelings of loss and a poignant reminder of what was.
- **Missing the version of yourself that existed in that relationship.** Within the dynamic of your marriage, you likely embodied certain roles and expressed particular aspects of your personality. You might have been the primary caregiver, the social planner, the adventurous one, or the pragmatic partner. When the marriage ends, you might find

yourself missing those familiar ways of being, even if the relationship wasn't entirely fulfilling. It's a natural part of grieving the life you once knew.

Gentle Truth: It's perfectly okay to grieve the "we" that was such a significant part of your life. Allow yourself the space to acknowledge those feelings of loss and the changes in your daily routines and identity. At the same time, try to gently embrace the opportunity to rediscover and celebrate the "me" that still exists within you, perhaps now with more clarity and freedom than before.

To help you explore this further, consider this exercise:

Exercise: The Identity Inventory

Take a piece of paper and fold it in half.

- On one side, under the heading **"Roles I've lost,"** list the roles you identified with within your marriage that no longer apply (e.g., "spouse," "husband/wife," "in-law," "co-host," "travel buddy").
- On the other side, under the heading **"Roles I still have or want,"** list the roles that remain important to you or that you wish to cultivate in this new chapter (e.g., "artist," "adventurer," "friend," "parent," "writer," "independent thinker").

Notice: Which side of the paper feels heavier? Does one side evoke more sadness or a sense of emptiness? Which side feels more alive, more aligned with the person you are now or aspire to be? This simple inventory can offer valuable insights into the aspects of your identity that have been impacted by the divorce and the areas where you can focus your energy as you rebuild your sense of self on this blank canvas. Remember, this is a journey of rediscovery, and you have the opportunity to paint a vibrant and authentic picture of who you are now and who you want to become.

Archaeology of the Self – Excavating Your Core

Think of your essential self as the foundation of a beautiful building. Over the years of your marriage, various layers might have been added – shared experiences, compromises, and the roles you played within the relationship. While these layers were significant, they didn't fundamentally alter the core structure beneath. Now, with the dissolution of the marriage, it's as if some of those outer layers have been removed, creating a unique opportunity to engage in an "archaeology of the self," gently excavating and rediscovering the core of who you truly are. This process is about uncovering the authentic you that has always existed, perhaps waiting patiently beneath the surface.

Here are some ways to begin this fascinating exploration:

1. Reconnect With Pre-Marriage You:

Think back to the person you were before you entered the marriage. What were your passions, your dreams, your unique quirks?

- **What did you love at 16 that you set aside?** Consider the hobbies, interests, or subjects that ignited your enthusiasm during your teenage years. Perhaps you were passionate about painting, playing a specific sport, writing poetry, or stargazing. Sometimes, in the busyness of life and relationships, these early loves can get pushed aside. Reconnecting with them now can bring a sense of joy and remind you of intrinsic parts of your identity.

- **What dreams did you label "unrealistic" for the relationship?** Were there aspirations you held – perhaps related to travel, career, or personal development – that felt incompatible with your married life or your partner's vision? Now is the time to revisit those dreams, to dust them off and consider if they still hold meaning for you. You might find that what once seemed unrealistic is now within the realm of possibility.

- **What quirky habit did you suppress to keep the peace?** We all have our little idiosyncrasies, those unique habits that make us who we are. Sometimes, in a relationship, we might consciously or unconsciously suppress these quirks to avoid conflict or fit in. Allow yourself to embrace those authentic parts of yourself again. They are what make you uniquely you.

Try This: Dedicate an afternoon to doing something your younger self adored. If you love spending time in nature, go for a hike. If you were a voracious reader, lose yourself in a book. This simple act can be a powerful way to reconnect with the essence of who you were before the layers of the marriage were built. Aha moment: Realizing that core aspects of your identity and passions might have been dormant but are still a vibrant and vital part of who you are.

2. Identify What Actually Feels Like You:

Post-divorce offers a fresh perspective and a chance to critically examine the beliefs, preferences, and even your personal style that you might have adopted or adapted within your marriage. This is your opportunity to conduct a personal audit:

- **Beliefs:** Take some time to reflect on the values and beliefs you held within your marriage. Do you still wholeheartedly agree with them? Or were some of these beliefs adopted to align with your partner's views? Now, you have the freedom to reaffirm your own core values and beliefs, independent of external influences.

- **Preferences:** Consider your tastes in various areas, such as music, art, food, and entertainment. Did you genuinely enjoy those things, or were they preferences you shared with or adopted from your ex-partner? Allow yourself to explore what truly resonates with you now without any obligation to share tastes.

- **Style:** Look at your personal style, from your wardrobe to your home decor. Does it truly reflect who you are today, or was it influenced by the "us" you projected as a couple? This is a chance to embrace a style that feels authentically you, one that makes you feel comfortable and confident in your own skin.

Small Rebellion: Change one thing about your environment – perhaps get a new haircut, rearrange your furniture, or buy yourself something you truly love – just because you want to. This small act of self-expression can be surprisingly liberating. Aha moment: Gaining clarity on your authentic likes, dislikes, and values, separate from the influences and compromises of the marriage.

3. Meet Your Present Self with Curiosity:

Engage in daily self-inquiry. Treat yourself with the same curiosity and openness you would extend to a new friend. Ask yourself:

- **What do I need today?** This simple question encourages you to tune into your current emotional, physical, and mental needs. Are you craving rest, connection, solitude, or activity? Honoring your needs is a fundamental act of self-care.

- **What's one small joy I can give myself?** This prompt encourages intentional acts of self-kindness. It could be anything from savoring a cup of coffee in silence to taking a walk in nature. These small moments of joy can significantly uplift your spirits.

- **What boundaries feel right to me now?** Your boundaries might have shifted since your marriage ended. What feels comfortable and healthy for you in terms of your time, energy, and emotional space? Re-evaluating and honoring your boundaries are crucial for your well-being.

Aha moment: Understanding the value of ongoing self-reflection and adapting to your present needs, recognizing that your identity is fluid and ever-evolving.

This journey of excavating your core self is a gentle process of uncovering and rediscovering the authentic you that has always been there. Embrace it with patience and kindness, allowing yourself the freedom to explore and redefine who you are now.

Trying On New Selves; The Freedom to Experiment

As you navigate this journey of rediscovering who you are after divorce, it's important to remember that rebuilding your identity isn't about suddenly constructing a flawless, brand-new version of yourself overnight. Instead, think of this time as an opportunity to embrace a sense of playful exploration, a chance to try on new selves without the pressure of long-term commitment or the expectation of immediate perfection. This is your permission slip to experiment, to discover what resonates with you now, without judgment or rigid plans.

Here are some ways to embrace this liberating phase:

1. Dabble Without Commitment:

This is your time to explore interests and activities simply because they pique your curiosity, without feeling the need to become an expert or make it a lifelong pursuit.

- **Take a class on something you've never tried.** Have you always been curious about pottery, creative writing, a new language, or a particular style of dance? Now is the perfect time to sign up for an introductory class. The beauty here is that there's no pressure to become a master. If you try it and discover it's not for you? Great, now you know, and you've expanded your horizons.

- **Explore different hobbies.** Perhaps you've always wanted to try gardening, knitting, photography, or learning a new instrument. Gather some basic supplies or watch a few online tutorials and give it a go. The focus isn't on producing perfect results but on the joy of the process and the potential for discovering new passions.

- **Read books or listen to podcasts on topics that intrigue you.** Expand your intellectual landscape by delving into subjects you've never explored before. This can be a low-pressure way to discover new interests and perspectives that might resonate with your evolving self.

Aha moment: Realizing that this is a time for joyful exploration without the burden of expectation or the fear of failure. Every new experience, whether you love it or not, offers valuable insights into what resonates with you now.

2. Redefine Success:

The traditional markers of success, particularly those often tied to marriage and family life, might feel different now. This is your opportunity to create your own, more personal definition of what success looks like for you in this new chapter.

- **Maybe the "married with kids by 30" dream is gone.** It's okay to acknowledge that loss and to release yourself from societal timelines or expectations that no longer fit your reality.
- **What new metrics matter to you now?** Consider what truly brings you fulfillment and a sense of accomplishment. Perhaps your definition of success now includes the following:
  - **Peace:** Cultivating inner calm and reducing stress in your daily life.
  - **Creativity:** Expressing yourself through art, writing, music, or any other creative outlet.
  - **Freedom to travel:** Having the flexibility to explore new places and experiences.
  - **Personal growth:** Learning new skills, expanding your knowledge, or developing a deeper understanding of yourself.
  - **Meaningful connections:** Building strong and supportive relationships with friends and family.

Aha moment: Feeling empowered to define your own version of success based on your current values and aspirations rather than adhering to outdated or external expectations.

3. Normalize the Awkward Phase:

As you try on these new selves and explore unfamiliar territories, it's perfectly normal to feel a little clumsy or uncertain. This is a period of transition, and it's okay if things don't feel perfectly natural right away.

- **Feeling clumsy in this new skin?** That's not failure, it's growth. Think of it like learning a new dance. You might stumble a few times before you find your rhythm. Be patient and kind to yourself as you navigate these new experiences.
- **Embrace the "beginner's mind."** Allow yourself to be a novice, to ask questions, and to learn without the pressure of needing to be an expert immediately.
- **Remember that growth often happens outside of our comfort zone.** Feeling a little awkward can actually be a sign that you are stretching yourself and expanding your horizons.

Mantra: Repeat to yourself, "I don't have to have it all figured out yet." This simple affirmation can release the pressure to have all the answers and allow you to embrace the process of discovery. Aha moment: Recognizing that feeling a little awkward or uncertain is a natural and even positive part of growth and that you don't need to have all the answers right now.

This time of trying on new selves is a gift, a chance to explore the vastness of who you are and who you are becoming without the constraints of the past. Embrace the freedom to experiment, to redefine success on your own terms, and to be gentle with yourself through any moments of awkwardness. This is your journey of joyful discovery.

The Stories We Tell; Rewriting Your Narrative

The stories we tell ourselves about our lives have an immense power to shape our perceptions and our futures. After divorce, it's easy to feel like the narrative of your life has been hijacked, perhaps casting you in a role you didn't choose or focusing on aspects of the story that leave you feeling disempowered. You might feel like a side character in a drama where the plot takes an unexpected and unwanted turn. But the beautiful truth is that you have the power to reclaim the pen, to rewrite your narrative in a way that honors your strength, your resilience, and the new direction your life is taking.

Think of your life as an unfolding story and divorce as a significant plot twist. Now is the time to re-examine that twist, not from a place of blame or defeat but from a perspective of growth and potential. One helpful framework for this is the Hero's Journey, a common pattern found in myths and stories around the world, which can also be applied to our personal transformations.

Exercise: The Hero's Journey

Reframe your divorce story using the following elements:

- **The Call: What signaled that change was needed?** Think back to the period leading up to your divorce. What were the initial signs, the underlying feelings, or the pivotal moments that indicated a shift was necessary? This isn't about assigning blame but rather about recognizing the forces that prompted change in your life. Perhaps there was a growing sense of unhappiness, a fundamental difference in values, or a specific event that served as a catalyst. Recognizing "the call" acknowledges that change, even if painful, was initiated for a reason.

- **The Ordeal: What did you survive?** The divorce process itself is often a challenging and arduous journey. What were the specific difficulties you faced? What pain did you endure? What obstacles did you overcome – whether emotional, practical, financial, or logistical? Acknowledging "the ordeal" honors your strength and resilience in navigating a difficult period. You survived something significant, and that in itself is a testament to your inner fortitude.

- **The Return: What wisdom are you bringing into this new chapter?** This is where you focus on the positive lessons learned and the growth you've experienced as a result of your divorce. What insights have you gained about yourself, about relationships, about what you truly value in life? What new strengths have you discovered within yourself? "The Return" emphasizes the wisdom you are carrying forward, shaping who you are becoming. Perhaps you learned the importance of setting boundaries, the value of self-care, or the strength of your own independence.

Example:

Instead of telling yourself, "I failed at marriage," you can reframe it as, "The Call: I recognized that the marriage was no longer serving my well-being. The Ordeal: I navigated a difficult separation and the emotional pain of letting go. The Return: I learned how to honor my worth and prioritize my own happiness in a way I didn't before."

Aha moment: By consciously reframing your divorce story through the lens of the Hero's Journey, you can shift from feeling like a victim of circumstance to recognizing yourself as the resilient hero of your own evolving narrative, someone who has faced challenges and emerged with valuable wisdom.

Take some time to reflect on your own experience using this framework. What is your call? What ordeal did you survive? What wisdom are you now carrying into this new chapter? As you begin to rewrite your narrative, focusing on your strength, your resilience, and the lessons you've learned, you will find yourself reclaiming agency over your story and stepping into your future with a renewed sense of purpose and empowerment. Remember, you are the author of your life, and this is your opportunity to write a compelling new chapter.

When Others Don't Recognize the New You

As you embrace the process of becoming and stepping into your new identity after divorce, you might encounter a common and sometimes challenging experience: the people around you, even those who care about you, might not immediately recognize or fully understand the changes you've undergone. They might be holding onto an image of the "you" they knew within the context of your marriage, and as you evolve, their reactions can sometimes feel a little jarring or even invalidating. Please know that this is a natural part of the process, and it's okay if navigating these interactions feels a bit delicate.

Here are some ways you might navigate these moments when others' perceptions don't quite align with the "new you":

Navigating Reactions

You might hear well-meaning but perhaps slightly off-kilter comments. Here's how you could respond with grace and clarity:

- **"You've changed!"** → **"Yes. I needed to."** This simple and direct response can be incredibly powerful. It acknowledges their observation while firmly stating your own agency in your transformation. It subtly communicates that this change wasn't arbitrary but a necessary step in your personal growth. You could also add, "I'm feeling more like myself now," or "I'm embracing a new chapter."

- **"But you used to love..."** → **"I'm discovering new things now."** This response gently redirects the conversation from the past to the present and future. It highlights your ongoing journey of self-discovery and allows you to acknowledge your past preferences without being confined by them. You might elaborate with, "My tastes have evolved," or "I'm finding joy in different things these days."

Boundary Script

Sometimes, despite your gentle explanations, others might continue to project their old perceptions onto you or offer unsolicited advice based on who they thought you were. In these situations, having a simple boundary script can be helpful:

- "I appreciate your concern, but this feels right for me." This response acknowledges their perspective without needing to justify your choices or engage in lengthy explanations. It clearly sets a boundary while maintaining a respectful tone. You could also adapt this to specific situations, such as, "I appreciate you thinking of me as a couple, but I'm enjoying exploring things on my own right now," or "Thank you for your advice, but I'm navigating this in a way that feels best for me."

Here's a table summarizing these helpful phrases:

Others' Observation/Comment	Your Potential Response
"You've changed!"	"Yes. I needed to." / "I'm feeling more like myself now."
"But you used to love [activity/item]."	"I'm discovering new things now." / "My tastes have evolved."
Unsolicited advice/old perceptions	"I appreciate your concern, but this feels right for me."

It's important to remember that people's perceptions often lag behind our own internal changes. They might need time to adjust to the "new you," and that's okay. Their reactions might stem from a place of care, even if they don't quite understand your current journey.

Ultimately, your own validation of your growth and transformation is what truly matters. You don't need external approval to embrace the person you are becoming. Be patient with others as they adjust, but more importantly, be patient and compassionate with yourself. Trust the path you are on, and know that as long as your choices feel authentic and right for you, that's what truly counts. Your journey of becoming is a deeply personal one, and you are the one who gets to define who you are now.

Closing: The Art of Becoming

Identity, dear friend, isn't a rigid structure, a statue carved once and left untouched by the currents of time and experience. Instead, think of it as a river, constantly flowing, adapting to the terrain, and reshaping its banks with each passing season. Just like a river, your sense of self is dynamic, ever-evolving, and responding to the journey you are on.

There will be days, undoubtedly, when you'll find yourself looking back at the familiar shores of your past, perhaps missing the way the river flowed in those earlier times. You might feel a pang of nostalgia for the roles you once played and the sense of self that was intertwined with them. And that is perfectly natural. Allow yourself those moments of reflection and gentle remembrance.

But there will also be days, perhaps with increasing frequency, when you'll feel a thrill at the new currents carrying you forward, leading you to landscapes you never imagined. You'll discover hidden strengths, unearth forgotten passions, and embrace aspects of yourself that were perhaps lying dormant. This is the art of becoming, the beautiful and ongoing process of shaping your identity as you navigate this new phase of your life.

Remember these truths as you continue on your way:

- **You are not less for having loved and lost.** The experiences you shared the love you gave and received, have shaped you in profound ways. Even though that chapter has closed, the wisdom and growth you gained remain an integral part of who you are.
- **You are more for having chosen to begin again.** It takes immense courage to face the

unknown, to gather the pieces of yourself, and to intentionally step onto a new path. This act of choosing to begin again is a testament to your resilience and your unwavering spirit.

Your identity will continue to evolve, shaped by your experiences, your choices, and your inner wisdom. Embrace this fluidity, this constant state of becoming, with kindness and curiosity towards yourself. Trust the journey you are on, and know that you have the strength and the capacity to create a future that is authentic, fulfilling, and uniquely yours. The river of your life is flowing onward, and you are the one steering your course.

Reflection Questions: A Path to Self-Understanding

These reflection questions are designed to help you solidify the foundation of your evolving identity, take stock of the incredible growth you've experienced, and gently guide you towards the future you are creating for yourself. Take a quiet moment with each of these, allowing your honest thoughts and feelings to surface. There are no right or wrong answers here, only opportunities for deeper self-understanding and a stronger sense of who you are becoming.

What's one way I've grown that would surprise my past self? Think back to who you were before the divorce or even in the early days of navigating its aftermath. What is one significant way you have changed, evolved, or discovered a strength you didn't know you possessed? Perhaps you've become more assertive, more independent, or more attuned to your own needs. Maybe you've embraced a new hobby, developed a new perspective, or found a resilience you never imagined. Acknowledging this growth can be incredibly empowering and highlight just how far you've come on this journey of self-discovery. Consider what your past self might marvel at or find unexpected about the person you are today. Aha moment: Recognizing this growth can be a powerful affirmation of your strength and adaptability, showcasing how you've positively transformed through this experience.

If no one were watching, what would I love to try? This question invites you to tap into your most authentic desires, free from any external expectations or judgments. What activities, hobbies, or experiences have you been curious about but perhaps haven't pursued due to the constraints or dynamics of your marriage? What secret longings or quiet interests have you kept tucked away? Now is your time to consider what truly excites you, what sparks your curiosity, without worrying about anyone else's opinions or approval. This exploration can reveal hidden aspects of yourself and guide you towards new sources of joy and fulfillment. Aha moment: Realizing the freedom you now have to explore your own genuine interests and passions, unburdened by past constraints, can open up exciting new possibilities.

What's a word or phrase that captures who I'm becoming? This question encourages you to distill the essence of your evolving identity into a concise descriptor. What word or short phrase resonates with the person you are discovering yourself to be? Perhaps it's "independent," "resilient," "creative," "peaceful," "adventurous," or "authentically me." This isn't about locking yourself into a rigid definition but rather about identifying a guiding principle or a core feeling that encapsulates your current direction and aspirations. This word or phrase can serve as a touchstone as you continue to grow and evolve. Aha moment: Identifying this core word or phrase can provide a powerful sense of clarity and direction, solidifying your understanding of the new self you are embracing.

These reflections are like laying the bricks for a solid and authentic foundation for your future. By honestly engaging with these questions, you can gain a clearer understanding of your growth, your desires, and the unique individual you are becoming in this new chapter of your life.

Chapter 9:

Rekindling Hope

The Quiet Return of Light

It's vital to understand that this dawning of hope doesn't mean the absence of pain. You might still experience moments of profound sadness, waves of grief that wash over you unexpectedly, or pangs of longing for what was. The beauty of this returning hope lies in its ability to coexist with these feelings. It's not about erasing the past or pretending that you are completely "over it." Instead, it's about creating space alongside your sorrow for the possibility of something good to emerge once more. Think of it like a garden after a storm. The damage might still be visible, the ground still damp, but new shoots of green are beginning to push through the soil, a testament to the enduring power of life and renewal.

This hope that is now stirring within you is not the same as the perhaps unburdened optimism you might have felt before experiencing the complexities and heartache of divorce. This is a hope that has been tested, refined, and strengthened by fire. It carries with it the wisdom of your journey, the understanding of your own resilience, and a quiet determination to find light again, even after navigating such profound darkness. It's a grounded hope, one that acknowledges the realities of your experience but refuses to be defined solely by them. It's a whisper of possibility that says, "I have been through hard things, and I am still here. I am capable of finding joy again."

And indeed, there is still more for you. This new chapter, though it may feel uncertain now, holds the potential for new connections, for rediscovering passions, and for creating a life that truly aligns with who you are now. It might involve finding joy in unexpected places, building relationships that nourish your soul, or pursuing dreams that you had perhaps put on hold. This returning hope is the gentle nudge that encourages you to keep moving forward, to remain open to the possibilities that await you, even if they are not yet fully clear. Like a tenacious plant that can find its way through cracks in the pavement towards the sunlight, your inner hope has the strength to guide you towards brighter days.

This chapter is here to walk alongside you as you recognize and nurture this precious flicker of hope. We will explore practical ways to tend to it and help it grow stronger and more resilient. Know that this quiet return of light is a significant and beautiful step on your path towards healing and a fulfilling future. Embrace it with tenderness and allow it to gently illuminate the way forward, one breath, one moment, one day at a time. You are not alone, and the possibility of joy is indeed still very much alive within you.

What Hope Looks Like After Loss

Hope After Divorce Isn't What You Expect

The idea of hope after experiencing the profound loss of a marriage can feel complex, perhaps even contradictory, in the early stages. You might wonder what it truly means to hope again when a significant chapter of your life has closed. It's important to understand that hope after divorce often looks and feels different from the expectations we might have held in the past. Let's gently explore what hope truly embodies in this new context and dispel some common misconceptions.

Hope After Divorce Isn't What You Expect

It's easy to confuse hope with certain outcomes or feelings. Here's what hope after divorce is not:

- **Forgetting the past:** Hope doesn't demand that you erase the memories of your marriage or the love you once shared. It's not about pretending that those experiences never happened or that they were insignificant. Instead, hope can coexist with memories, both good and bad. It's about finding a way to carry the lessons and the love you experienced forward without being solely defined by the past. You can remember and even grieve what was while still holding onto the possibility of good things to come.

- **Pretending you're "over it":** Hope isn't about putting on a brave face and convincing yourself or others that you've completely moved on and are unaffected by the divorce. It's okay to still have moments of sadness, anger, or longing. Hope allows for the full spectrum of your emotions. It simply adds a gentle whisper that these feelings, while real, won't be your entire story forever. It acknowledges the present while still looking towards a future where those feelings might hold less power.

- **Blind faith that everything will be perfect:** Hope after loss isn't about naively believing that your life will suddenly become flawless and free from any future challenges. It's a more grounded and realistic perspective. It acknowledges that life will likely continue to have its ups and downs, but it maintains a fundamental belief in your ability to navigate those challenges and experience moments of joy and fulfillment along the way. It's about trusting in your own resilience, not in a fairytale ending.

It is:

- **The courage to believe in small good things again:** In the immediate aftermath of divorce, even the smallest joys might feel overshadowed by pain. Hope, in this context, is the quiet courage that allows you to open yourself up to the possibility of experiencing those small good things once more. It might be the warmth of the sun on your skin, a genuine laugh shared with a friend, the comfort of a good book, or the satisfaction of a simple accomplishment. It's about allowing yourself to notice and appreciate these moments, even if they feel fleeting at first.

- **Trusting that your capacity for joy hasn't been destroyed:** The pain of divorce can sometimes feel so profound that it might lead you to believe you'll never experience true happiness again. Hope gently reminds you that your capacity for joy is still within you, even if it feels dormant right now. It's about trusting that you will eventually be able to reconnect with that part of yourself, that the ability to feel joy hasn't been extinguished but is simply waiting for the right time and space to re-emerge.

- **Letting yourself imagine a future without flinching:** The idea of a future after divorce can be daunting, filled with uncertainty and perhaps even fear. Hope offers you the space to begin imagining that future, even if just in small glimpses, without immediately being overwhelmed by those negative emotions. It's about allowing yourself to entertain the possibility of new experiences, new connections, and a life that is fulfilling in ways you might not yet fully understand.

Reflection: "If hope were a color, what would it look like for me right now?" Take a moment to consider this question. What color comes to mind when you think about the feeling of hope in your current situation? Is it a bright, vibrant hue or perhaps a softer, more muted shade? There's no right or wrong answer. The color you choose can represent your personal understanding and feeling of hope at this moment in your journey. Consider the intensity of the color, any emotions it evokes, and what that might tell you about how hope is beginning to manifest in your life. This personal reflection can offer a valuable glimpse into your inner landscape and your evolving relationship with hope.

The Science of Hope

It can be incredibly reassuring to know that the return of hope after loss isn't just a whimsical idea or a fleeting emotion. Research in psychology has actually delved into the nature of hope, offering valuable insights that can feel validating and empowering as you navigate this time. Understanding the science behind hope can provide a solid foundation for actively nurturing it in your own life.

Here's what research shows us about this powerful aspect of the human experience:

- **A skill (not just a feeling) that can be cultivated:** This is a crucial understanding. Hope isn't simply a passive emotion that either appears or doesn't. Instead, it's a way of thinking and behaving that can be actively developed and strengthened, much like any other skill. This means that even if hope feels distant right now, you have the power to cultivate it. This might involve consciously setting small, achievable goals for yourself, practicing problem-solving when challenges arise, and engaging in positive self-talk that reinforces your ability to cope and move forward. Just as you might learn a new language or a musical instrument through practice, you can also learn to become more hopeful. *Aha moment: Recognizing that hope is an active skill puts you in the driver's seat, empowering you to take concrete steps towards fostering it in your life.*

- **Linked to better emotional and physical recovery:** Studies have shown a strong connection between hope and overall well-being, particularly in times of adversity. When you hold onto hope, it can positively impact both your emotional and physical recovery. Emotionally, hope can reduce feelings of stress, anxiety, and depression, fostering a more positive mood and a greater sense of inner peace. Physically, research suggests that hope can even contribute to better sleep, a stronger immune system, and an enhanced ability to cope with physical challenges. In the context of divorce, nurturing hope can significantly contribute to your healing process, helping you navigate the emotional complexities and rebuild your life with greater resilience. *Aha moment: Understanding the tangible benefits of hope for your overall healing can provide a powerful motivation to actively cultivate it.*

- **Built on two things: agency (belief in your ability to act) and pathways (seeing options ahead).** This is a core concept in the science of hope. Researchers have found that hope is built upon two key pillars:
  - **Agency (Belief in your ability to act):** This refers to your belief in your own capacity

to influence your future and to take actions that will lead to positive outcomes. After divorce, it's easy to feel powerless or like you're simply being carried along by circumstances. Cultivating agency involves recognizing your own inner strength and your ability to make choices that will improve your situation. This might involve taking small steps towards your goals, seeking support when you need it, or making decisions that align with your values and your vision for your future. *Aha moment: Recognizing your own agency reminds you that you are not a passive victim of circumstance but an active participant in shaping your own destiny.*

o **Pathways (Seeing options ahead):** This refers to your ability to envision different routes and strategies for achieving your goals and overcoming obstacles. When you're feeling hopeless, it can often feel like you're stuck with no way forward. Cultivating pathways involves brainstorming different possibilities, seeking advice from others, and being open to exploring new approaches. It's about recognizing that even when one path seems blocked, there are often other ways to reach your desired destination. This requires flexibility, creativity, and a willingness to consider different options. *Aha moment: Realizing that even when things feel bleak, there are often multiple ways forward, and* *you have the capacity to find those pathways.*

Understanding these scientific principles can empower you to approach hope not as a passive wish but as an active skill you can develop. By focusing on building your sense of agency and exploring the pathways ahead, you can intentionally cultivate hope and navigate your journey after divorce with greater strength and optimism.

Finding Your Embers; Where Hope Hides

There will be times on this journey when the return of hope feels like a distant dream, a faint whisper that's easily drowned out by the louder voices of sadness or uncertainty. In these moments, it's important to remember that hope often doesn't announce itself with fanfare. Instead, it tends to reside in the quiet corners of our lives and the world around us, waiting to be gently discovered. When hope feels impossible to grasp, try looking for its subtle presence in these unexpected places:

- **Your Body's Wisdom:** Your body is deeply connected to your emotional state, and often signals shifts in your inner landscape long before your conscious mind fully registers them. Pay attention to these subtle physical cues:
    - **In the morning, your shoulders feel slightly lighter:** Have you noticed a day where the persistent tension you've been carrying in your shoulders seems to ease, even just a little? This physical lightness can be a sign that some of the emotional weight

you've been bearing is beginning to lift, a quiet indication that the burden of grief is lessening, making space for a glimmer of hope. *Aha moment: Recognizing that your body can be a barometer for your emotional healing and even subtle physical ease can signal the return of hope.*

○ **The first time you crave a food you used to love:** Has a familiar craving for a food you once enjoyed suddenly resurfaced? This might seem like a small thing, but it can actually be a significant sign that your capacity for pleasure and enjoyment is reawakening. It suggests that the numbness that can accompany grief is starting to recede, allowing you to connect with simple joys once more. *Aha moment: Seeing the return of simple pleasures like a favorite food as a tangible sign that hopes and the ability to experience joy are returning to your life.*

○ **The deep sigh after a good cry that somehow leaves you calmer:** While tears can be an expression of sadness, they can also be incredibly cathartic. Notice the feeling after a good cry, that sense of release that somehow leaves you feeling a little bit calmer, a little less burdened. This release is a sign that you are processing your emotions, and with each wave, you might find yourself moving closer to a place of acceptance and eventual peace. *Aha moment: Understanding that even within sadness, there can be moments of release that pave* *the way for a sense of calm and the quiet emergence of hope.*

- **Nature's Cycles:** The natural world is a constant reminder of resilience, renewal, and the enduring cycle of life. Observing nature can offer profound comfort and a sense of hope, even in the midst of personal turmoil:
    - **The stubborn flower growing through a crack in concrete:** Have you ever noticed a vibrant flower pushing its way through seemingly impenetrable concrete? This is a powerful metaphor for the resilience of life, the inherent drive to survive and even thrive against the odds. It's a reminder that even in the most challenging circumstances, beauty and strength can emerge. *Aha moment: Seeing nature as a powerful symbol of enduring strength and the unwavering possibility of thriving even after experiencing significant hardship.*
    - **The way trees lose leaves only to regrow them:** The cyclical nature of trees, shedding their leaves in the fall only to burst forth with new growth in the spring, is a beautiful illustration of renewal and the promise of new beginnings. It reminds us that endings are often followed by fresh starts and that even after a period of loss, there is always the potential for growth and new life. *Aha moment: Finding comfort and hope in the cyclical nature of life, recognizing that even after the "winter" of divorce, a "spring" of new possibilities will eventually arrive.*

- o **The certainty that dawn always follows night:** This fundamental truth of nature offers a powerful and unwavering symbol of hope. No matter how dark the night may seem, the dawn will always eventually break. This certainty reminds us that even the most difficult periods will eventually give way to light and a new beginning. *Aha moment: Connecting with the universal and comforting truth that even the darkest times eventually give way to light and the promise of a new day, bringing with it renewed possibilities for hope.*

Practice: Make it a point to spend at least 10 minutes outside each day. During this time, consciously try to notice one small sign of resilience in nature. It could be a bird singing, a plant pushing through the soil, or the changing colors of the sky.

- **Others' Stories:** Connecting with the experiences of others who have navigated similar challenges can be a powerful source of hope and encouragement:
  - o **The friend who survived divorce and now thrives:** Do you know someone who has gone through a divorce and has emerged on the other side, living a fulfilling and happy life? Their story can be an incredibly potent source of inspiration, demonstrating that it is indeed possible to not only survive but to truly thrive after the end of a marriage. *Aha moment: Gaining tangible hope and encouragement from witnessing firsthand that others have successfully navigated this journey and built fulfilling new lives.*

- The memoir makes you think, "If they made it, maybe I can too" Reading the stories of others who have faced similar hardships and found their way to healing and hope can create a powerful sense of connection and possibility. It reminds you that you are not alone in your struggles and that the path to healing, while unique to each individual, is one that many have successfully traversed. *Aha moment: Finding solace and a sense of possibility in connecting with the shared human experience of overcoming adversity, realizing that if others have found their way, you can, too.*

- The stranger's kindness that reminds you of goodness still exists: Even small, unexpected acts of kindness from strangers can serve as powerful reminders that there is still goodness and compassion in the world, even when your personal world might feel fractured. These moments can reaffirm your faith in humanity and offer a glimmer of hope for the future. *Aha moment: Being reminded that despite personal pain and loss, kindness and goodness are still prevalent in the world around you, offering a sense of connection and hope.*

Exercise: Create a "Hope Collection." This could be a physical or digital collection of quotes, song lyrics, images, or short stories that spark a feeling of warmth, resilience, or hope within you. When you're feeling discouraged, revisit your collection as a gentle reminder that light can always be found, even in the darkest of times.

Nurturing the Flame – Practical Ways to Cultivate Hope

The ember of hope that might be flickering within you after the darkness of divorce needs gentle tending and consistent nourishment to grow into a steady flame. Just like a precious plant, hope thrives with care and attention. Here are some practical and accessible ways you can actively cultivate and strengthen hope in your daily life:

- **The "Even If" Exercise:** This simple yet powerful exercise can help to gently open your mind to possibilities, even when doubt feels overwhelming.

  - Complete the sentence: "Even if I don't believe it yet, I'm open to the possibility that..."
  - The key here is the phrase "even if I don't believe it yet." This acknowledges any current feelings of skepticism or despair, allowing you to approach the possibility of hope without pressure. It's about creating a small crack in the door of negativity to let a sliver of light in.
  - Here are some examples to get you started:

    - "...I could feel genuine happiness again."
    - "...I could build a fulfilling and joyful life on my own."
    - "...I could find new connections and friendships that truly nourish me."

- "...I could discover new passions and interests that excite me."
- "...I could find peace and acceptance about the past."
- "...I could learn and grow from this experience."

  o Practice completing this sentence regularly, even if the words feel difficult to say or believe at first. Over time, you might find that the "even if" starts to feel less like a disclaimer and more like a gentle opening to a brighter future. ***Aha moment:*** *Recognizing that even a small willingness to consider positive possibilities can begin to shift your mindset towards hope, even when your current feelings suggest otherwise.*

- **Small Future Trips:** Planning something to look forward to, no matter how small, can create a sense of anticipation and provide a gentle nudge of hope in your daily life. Think of these as little anchors in time that you can look towards with a sense of positive expectation.

  o **A movie release next month:** Mark your calendar for a film you've been wanting to see. This gives you a concrete event to anticipate and enjoy.
  o **A coffee date with a friend:** Schedule a casual get-together with someone whose company you enjoy. Connection and conversation can be powerful mood boosters.

- Trying a new recipe this weekend: Experimenting in the kitchen can be a fun and rewarding way to engage your senses and create something positive for yourself.
- **Visiting a local attraction, you've never been to:** Explore your surroundings and discover something new in your own community.
- **Planning a self-care day:** Dedicate a day to activities that nourish your mind, body, and soul, whether it's a long bath, reading a good book, or spending time in nature.
- The scale of the "trip" doesn't matter; what's important is having something positive on your horizon to look forward to. *Aha moment: Understanding that even small, planned, enjoyable events can create a sense of purpose and inject moments of light and hope into your present experience.*

- **Hope Anchors:** Creating tangible reminders of hope can provide comfort and strength during moments of doubt or discouragement. These anchors can serve as physical representations of your intention to cultivate hope.

  - **A playlist titled "Glimmers":** Curate a collection of songs that evoke feelings of hope, resilience, peace, or joy for you. Music has a powerful way of tapping into our emotions and can be a readily accessible source of comfort and inspiration. Listen to your "Glimmers" playlist when you need a boost of positivity. *Aha moment:*

Recognizing the emotional power of music and intentionally using it as a tangible reminder of hope and positive feelings.

o **A hope jar (add notes when good things happen):** Find a jar and keep it in a visible place. Whenever something good happens, no matter how small, write it down on a slip of paper and put it in the jar. On days when hope feels distant, take out a few notes and remind yourself of the positive moments you've experienced. *Aha moment: Seeing the accumulation of positive experiences, even small ones, as a tangible testament to the presence of goodness and hope in your life.*

o **A wristband you touch when doubt creeps in:** Choose a simple wristband or another small physical item that you can wear or keep with you. When feelings of doubt, fear, or negativity arise, touch this anchor as a conscious reminder of your intention to cultivate hope and your inner strength. *Aha moment: Realizing the grounding and reassuring effect of having a physical reminder that you can connect with during challenging emotional moments.*

By consistently engaging with these practical exercises, you can actively nurture the flame of hope within you, helping it to grow stronger and brighter with each passing day. Remember to be patient and kind to yourself throughout this process. Cultivating hope takes time and effort, but the rewards – a greater sense of peace, resilience, and optimism – are well worth it.

When Hope Feels Like Betrayal

As the gentle warmth of hope begins to thaw the frozen landscape of your heart after divorce, it's not uncommon for a wave of complex and sometimes conflicting emotions to surface. You might find yourself questioning this newfound lightness, wondering if allowing yourself to envision a brighter future somehow diminishes the significance of the past or disrespects the pain you've endured. This feeling of hope being akin to betrayal is a natural and understandable part of the healing process. It speaks to the depth of your commitment to the marriage and the sincerity of your grief.

Here are some Common Fears that might surface when hope begins to peek through, along with a deeper exploration of these feelings:

- **"If I hope again, does that mean my marriage meant nothing?"** This fear strikes at the core of your past experiences and the love you once shared. It's as if allowing yourself to be happy again would somehow invalidate the time, effort, and emotions you invested in your marriage. But think of it like this: enjoying a delicious new meal doesn't erase the pleasure you derived from your favorite dish in the past. Each experience holds its own value. Your marriage was a significant part of your life, filled with its own joys and lessons. Hoping for a fulfilling future doesn't negate that history; it simply acknowledges your inherent right to happiness and growth moving forward. It honors your capacity to love and be loved, which remains within you regardless of the past. *Aha moment: Recognizing that hope for the future and honoring the memories* *and lessons of the past can beautifully coexist without diminishing each other.*

- **"What if I hope and get hurt again?"** This fear is a natural response to having experienced the pain of a broken relationship. The vulnerability of allowing yourself to feel optimistic about the future can feel risky as if you're setting yourself up for potential disappointment. It's important to acknowledge this fear and the wisdom it carries from your past. However, hope isn't about guaranteeing a pain-free future. Life inevitably has its challenges. Instead, hope is about choosing to remain open to the possibility of joy, connection, and fulfillment, even with the awareness that future difficulties might arise. Your past experiences have likely made you stronger and more attuned to your own needs, equipping you with valuable insights for navigating future relationships. ***Aha moment:*** *Understanding that hope isn't about denying the possibility of future hurt but about having the courage to remain open to joy and positive experiences despite past pain, armed with newfound wisdom and resilience.*

Here are some **Mantras for the Weary Heart** to gently guide you through these complex emotions:

- **"I can miss what was and still want what will be."** This mantra beautifully encapsulates the idea that grief and hope can coexist. It's okay to feel sadness for the loss of your marriage and to cherish the memories you hold while simultaneously yearning for and being open to the good things that the future might hold. These two feelings are not mutually exclusive; they are both valid parts of your human experience. ***Aha moment:*** *Feeling validated in experiencing the duality of emotions – both missing the past and desiring a positive future – without judgment or inner conflict.*

- **"Hope isn't a certainty, and it's courage."** Remind yourself that hope is not a guarantee of a perfect outcome or a life free from challenges. Rather, it's an act of bravery, especially after experiencing heartbreak and uncertainty. Choosing to be hopeful is a conscious decision to lean into possibility, even when you don't have all the answers or assurances. It's a testament to your strength and your willingness to believe in a brighter tomorrow despite the risks. ***Aha moment:*** *Reframing hope as an act of courage and inner strength, empowering you to embrace it even in the face of uncertainty.*

- **"My past pain makes my hope more precious, not less valid."** Your journey through divorce, including the pain you've endured, has likely given you a deeper appreciation for the good things in life and a clearer understanding of what truly matters to you. Your hope for the future is not diminished by your past experiences; in fact, it can be even more meaningful because it is born from a place of profound understanding, resilience, and a deep desire for happiness. Your past pain has refined your capacity for joy, making your hope all the more valuable. ***Aha moment:*** *Recognizing that your past pain doesn't disqualify you from future hope; instead, it can deepen your appreciation for joy and make your hope even more precious and meaningful.*

It's also important to allow yourself to forgive yourself for hoping again. There might be a sense of guilt associated with moving forward, but remember that healing and growth are natural and healthy responses to life's challenges. Embracing hope is not a betrayal; it's an act of self-compassion and a testament to your enduring spirit.

The Ripple Effects of Hope

As that quiet flame of hope within you begins to grow stronger, you might be surprised by the positive ripples that extend into various aspects of your life. Cultivating hope isn't just about feeling a bit more optimistic; it can have tangible and beneficial effects on your physical well-being, your emotional landscape, and your connections with the world around you. Let's go into some of these beautiful ripple effects:

- **Physically:** As hope takes root, you might notice a subtle but significant shift in your physical energy levels. The heavy fatigue that can often accompany grief and despair might begin to lift, replaced by a renewed sense of vitality. You might find yourself with **more energy** to engage in activities you once enjoyed or to simply navigate your day with greater ease. Furthermore, hope can often lead to **better sleep**. The anxieties and worries that can keep you awake at night might lessen as you begin to feel more secure in the possibility of a positive future, allowing for more restful and restorative sleep. *Aha moment: Recognizing that nurturing hope can have direct and positive impacts on your physical health and energy levels, contributing to your overall well-being.*

- **Emotionally:** The growth of hope can bring about a gentle but profound transformation in your emotional landscape. You might find yourself experiencing **fewer spirals** into negativity or despair. While moments of sadness or grief might still arise, they may not feel as overwhelming or as likely to consume you. Instead, you might notice **more moments of peace** and a greater sense of inner calm. Hope acts as a gentle anchor, helping to steady your emotions and providing a sense of resilience in the face of challenges. *Aha moment: Witnessing how hope gradually shifts your emotional patterns, bringing more moments of tranquility and reducing the intensity of negative feelings.*

- **Relationally:** As your own inner light of hope grows brighter, it can naturally draw people towards you who resonate with that positive energy. You might find yourself attracting individuals who are supportive, understanding, and who reflect your own growing sense of optimism. This isn't about suddenly becoming someone you're not but rather about the subtle ways in which your own hopeful outlook can influence the kinds of connections you make and nurture. You might find yourself building **healthier future connections** with people who uplift and encourage you on your journey. *Aha moment: Realizing that your own internal hopefulness can have a positive influence on your relationships, attracting people who align with your evolving self.*

Consider this Story Spot: "After my divorce, I planted bulbs in winter. It felt like a small act of faith in a future spring I couldn't yet see. When they bloomed in vibrant colors months later, I realized I'd been growing too." This simple yet powerful story beautifully illustrates the ripple effects of hope. The act of planting those bulbs was an expression of hope for the future. As the bulbs grew beneath the surface, unseen, so too was the individual undergoing their own process of growth and healing. The eventual blooming was a tangible manifestation of that hope and inner transformation.

Just as planting a seed can led to a beautiful bloom, nurturing hope within yourself can lead to profound and positive changes in your life. Embrace these ripple effects, recognizing them as gentle signs of your healing and your journey towards a brighter tomorrow.

Closing: The Bravest Thing You'll Do

In the aftermath of heartbreak, especially after the profound experience of divorce, allowing yourself to hope again might feel like a vulnerable and even daunting prospect. But please know, dear friend, that hope after heartbreak isn't foolish. In fact, it is one of the most courageous acts you can undertake. To believe in the possibility of light after knowing darkness so intimately, to open your heart to the potential for joy after experiencing such deep sorrow – that is an act of immense bravery.

Some days, your hope might feel like a roaring bonfire, burning brightly with a clear vision of a positive future. You might feel a surge of optimism and a strong sense of anticipation for all the good things to come. Embrace those days and let that warmth sustains you.

But there will also be days when your hope feels more like a single match struck in the wind, a tiny flicker of light that you must shield carefully to prevent it from being extinguished by lingering doubts or sadness. On those days, please remember that even that small spark is enough. It signifies that the possibility is still there, that the flame hasn't gone out entirely, and that with gentle care, it can grow stronger.

Here are some key takeaways to remember:

- **Courage in Vulnerability:** Choosing hope after heartbreak requires vulnerability, and vulnerability is a sign of strength, not weakness.
- **Every Flicker Counts:** Whether your hope feels like a bonfire or a single match, acknowledge and cherish its presence. Every bit of hope is valuable.
- **Your Story Continues:** As long as that flame of hope flickers within you, no matter how small, it means your story isn't over. New chapters are waiting to be written.

You have already demonstrated incredible strength in navigating the challenges of divorce. Now, as you allow hope to re-enter your heart, you are embarking on another courageous journey – the journey towards healing and a brighter future. Trust in your resilience, be kind to yourself, and know that even the smallest spark of hope has the power to guide you forward. You are brave, and the light within you is ready to shine again.

Reflection Questions: A Path to Self-Understanding

These reflection questions are gentle prompts to help you connect with the returning flame of hope within you and to actively tend to its growth. Take a few quiet moments to consider each one, allowing your honest thoughts and feelings to surface. There are no right or wrong answers, only opportunities for deeper self-awareness and a stronger connection to your own inner resilience.

What's one small thing that felt hopeful this week? As you reflect on the past few days, try to recall even a tiny instance that sparked a sense of hope within you. It might have been a brief moment of lightness that lifted your spirits, a feeling of anticipation for something positive on the horizon, or a simple reminder that good things are still possible in your life. Perhaps a friend reached out with particularly encouraging words, you accomplished a small task that felt surprisingly significant, you witnessed an act of kindness, or you simply enjoyed the beauty of a sunrise or a peaceful moment in nature. Acknowledging these small glimmers of hope, no matter how fleeting they might seem, helps to reinforce their presence in your life and gently encourages you to look for them more actively in the days ahead. Aha moment: Recognizing even the smallest instances that sparked hope can illuminate the subtle ways positivity is returning to your life, building momentum for a brighter outlook.

When have I overcome something hard before? How did hope help? Think back to a challenging time in your life, perhaps even before your divorce or perhaps a difficult moment earlier in your healing journey. What was the specific situation, and how did you navigate through it? Can you recall any moments when hope, even if it was just a tiny spark flickering within you, played a role in your ability to persevere and keep moving forward? Maybe it was the hope of a better future, the hope of finding a solution to a seemingly insurmountable problem, or simply the hope of making it through another difficult day. Reflecting on your past resilience and the specific ways in which hope, in any form, supported you through those tough times can serve as a powerful reminder of your inner strength and your innate capacity to overcome difficulties, fostering a renewed sense of hope for your current journey as well. Aha moment: Connecting your past experiences of overcoming adversity with the power of hope can reinforce your inherent resilience and strengthen your belief in navigating your current challenges.

If hope could speak to me today, what would it say? Take a quiet moment to tune into your inner self, to that gentle and intuitive voice within. Imagine for a moment that the feeling of hope itself could speak to you directly in this very moment. What message might it offer? Would it be a message of reassurance, gently reminding you that you are stronger than you currently believe? Would it encourage you to be patient with yourself and to trust the natural unfolding of the healing process? Or perhaps it would whisper about the exciting possibilities that lie ahead, just waiting to be discovered? Allowing yourself to connect with this inner sense of hope, to personify it and listen for its gentle guidance, can provide profound comfort, renewed strength, and a sense of possibility as you continue to tend to your own precious returning flame. Aha moment: Connecting with your inner sense of hope and imagining its message can provide personalized guidance and reassurance that resonates deeply with your current needs and aspirations.

Chapter 10:

Embracing Solitude

The Space Between Loneliness and Liberation

The experience of divorce often brings with it a stark shift in your physical surroundings and daily routines. Rooms that once echoed with shared laughter and conversation might now feel quiet and empty. Mornings that used to begin with the comforting presence of another, might now unfold in a stillness that feels both unfamiliar and profound. It's in these moments, surrounded by this newfound quiet, that the distinction between being alone and feeling truly lonely becomes incredibly important.

In the immediate aftermath of divorce, it's completely natural for this solitude to feel like a form of abandonment. The silence can be deafening, a constant reminder of the companionship that is no longer there. Empty spaces in your home might feel like hollow echoes of what was lost, and the quiet of your own company might initially feel like a heavy weight, a stark contrast to the shared life you once knew. This feeling of being alone can easily morph into a deep sense of loneliness, a yearning for connection and a painful awareness of the absence of your former partner.

But within this very same space, this quiet and solitude lies an unexpected potential. If you allow yourself to approach it with openness and a willingness to explore, this time alone can transform into something quite different, something akin to the sacred ground for the essential work of rediscovering yourself. It's a space where the noise of the partnership fades, allowing your own inner voice to become clearer.

This chapter isn't here to suggest that solitude is always easy or that the pangs of loneliness will never arise. We acknowledge that the ache of missing someone, of longing for connection, is a real and valid part of this journey. Instead, our focus will be on uncovering the unique gifts that only solitude can offer. It's in these quiet moments that you have the precious opportunity to truly hear your own thoughts again without the filters or compromises that often come with being in a relationship. It's a chance to remember what truly brings you joy, independent of shared interests or external expectations. And perhaps most importantly, it's an invaluable time to rebuild and nurture a deeper, more authentic relationship with the most important person in your life – you. This space, initially perceived as a void, can become a sanctuary for self-discovery and a pathway towards a profound sense of liberation.

The Alchemy of Alone – Transforming Loneliness Into Solitude

In navigating the landscape after divorce, one of the most crucial distinctions to understand is the difference between loneliness and solitude. While they might both involve spending time on your own, the inner experience of each is vastly different. Recognizing this distinction is the first step in transforming what might feel like a painful absence into a powerful opportunity for self-discovery.

Let's explore the nuances between these two states:

Loneliness	Solitude
Feels like something is missing	Feels like something is being found
Heavy, aching	Light, spacious
"I wish someone were here."	"I'm glad to be here with myself."

When you're feeling lonely after divorce, there's often a sense of yearning, a feeling that something essential is absent from your life. It can feel heavy and aching, accompanied by the persistent thought, "I wish someone were here to share this with me." This feeling can be particularly strong when facing moments or situations that you once shared with your former partner.

Solitude, on the other hand, while also involving being alone, carries a different energy. It can feel like a welcome space where you are actively finding something – perhaps peace, clarity, or a deeper connection with yourself. Solitude can feel light and spacious, offering a sense of freedom and the quiet affirmation, "I'm glad to be here with myself." It's a conscious choice to embrace your own company and find value in your time alone.

Note: It's important to remember that it's perfectly normal to oscillate between these two feelings. Some moments of being alone might feel liberating and restorative, while others might trigger pangs of loneliness. The goal isn't to feel lonely, that's a natural human emotion, but rather to allow solitude to exist alongside it, to find moments of peace and self-connection even when the ache of loneliness surfaces.

So, why can solitude feel so scary, especially after the significant loss of a marriage? Here are a few reasons:

- **Your brain is wired for connection; absence triggers primal stress.** As human beings, we are inherently social creatures. Our brains are wired for connection, and the absence of close relationships can trigger primal stress responses. After the consistent companionship of marriage, being alone can feel like a threat to our sense of safety and well-being, even if we consciously desire some time for ourselves.

- **Society equates being alone with being "unwanted"** Unfortunately, societal narratives often equate being alone with being "unwanted" or "failed." This can be particularly amplified after divorce, leading to feelings of shame or inadequacy about your single status. It's important to challenge these negative societal messages and recognize that choosing solitude, even if initially circumstantial, can be a powerful act of self-care and a necessary step in your healing.

- **You may have forgotten who you are outside of a "we"** As we discussed in the previous chapter, marriage often involves a blending of identities. After divorce, you might find yourself grappling with the question of who you are now, independent of your former partner. Solitude can feel daunting when you haven't yet reconnected with your individual identity and your own unique preferences and desires.

Gentle Truth: What if this solitude you're experiencing isn't a punishment or a sign of being unwanted but rather a homecoming? What if it's an opportunity to finally reconnect with the essential you, the person who might have been a bit overshadowed within the dynamic of your marriage? By reframing your perspective, you can begin to see the potential for profound self-discovery and growth within this space of being alone. This alchemy of alone – transforming loneliness into solitude – is about shifting your focus from what's missing to what can be found within yourself.

The Gifts Only Solitude Can Give

While the initial quiet of solitude after divorce might feel unsettling, it holds within it a treasure trove of unique gifts, opportunities for healing and growth that can be found nowhere else. Embracing this time alone, even amidst moments of loneliness, can lead to a deeper understanding of yourself and a stronger foundation for your future. Let's get into some of these invaluable gifts:

Hearing Your Own Voice Again: In the natural rhythm of a relationship, there's often a blending of voices, a series of compromises and shared decisions. Solitude offers a precious opportunity to reconnect with your own inner voice, the one that might have been quieted or muted within the dynamic of your marriage.

- Without the noise of a relationship's compromises, you can Rediscover opinions you might have subconsciously set aside to maintain harmony or align with your partner's views. Now, you have the space to truly explore what you think and believe without the need for external validation or agreement.
- Notice what you truly enjoy (not what you learned to tolerate): Shared activities and interests are a beautiful part of the partnership, but sometimes they can overshadow our individual preferences. Solitude allows you to rediscover what truly brings *you* joy, whether it's a particular genre of music, a type of food, or a way of spending your free time that might have been less appealing to your former partner.
- Trust your instincts without second-guessing: When you're accustomed to considering another person's perspective in every decision, it can be easy to second-guess your own instincts. Solitude provides the space to reconnect with your intuition and build confidence in your own judgment, allowing you to make choices based on what feels right for you.

Exercise: Spend a day saying "yes" or "no" to things based solely on your own desire, without considering anyone else's needs or expectations. Notice how this feels and what it reveals about your authentic preferences. Aha moment: Recognizing the clarity and freedom that comes from tuning into your own inner voice and honoring your individual desires.

The Luxury of Unobserved Being: There's a profound liberation in simply being yourself without the feeling of being watched or needing to explain your actions or moods. Solitude offers this unique and valuable space.

- Solitude lets you Dance badly to your favorite song at the top of your lungs without a hint of self-consciousness. Eat cereal for dinner in your pajamas without needing to justify your choices. Sit in comfortable silence, simply being with your own thoughts and feelings, without feeling the need to fill the quiet or explain your mood.
- This is a time to shed any expectations of how you "should" be and simply embrace who you are in that moment, without performance or explanation. It's about finding comfort and acceptance in your own skin, exactly as you are.

Mantra: Repeat to yourself, "I am free to take up space exactly as I am." Aha moment: Appreciating the liberating feeling of simply being yourself without any external pressures or the need for validation.

Depth Over Distraction: In the hustle and bustle of daily life, especially within a partnership, it can be challenging to find the quiet space needed for deeper reflection and processing. Solitude provides this invaluable opportunity.

- Alone time fosters:
  - Creativity: With fewer external distractions, your mind has the space to wander and explore new ideas. Journaling, painting, writing, or simply allowing your thoughts to flow freely can lead to surprising creative breakthroughs and a deeper understanding of your inner world.
  - Spiritual connection: Solitude creates the stillness needed for practices like meditation,

mindfulness, or simply spending time in nature, allowing you to connect with a sense of something larger than yourself and explore your spiritual beliefs.

○ Emotional processing: It's in quiet moments alone that you can truly allow yourself to feel your emotions fully, whether it's tears, sadness, anger, or joy. This dedicated time for emotional processing can lead to profound breakthroughs, clarity, and a greater sense of inner peace.

Try This: Light a candle in a quiet room and ask yourself, "What do I need to feel at peace today?" Allow yourself to sit with the question and see what insights or feelings arise. Aha moment: Recognizing the profound opportunity for deeper self-understanding, creative exploration, and spiritual connection that solitude provides.

These gifts of solitude are not just about filling empty time; they are about actively engaging with yourself in ways that foster healing, growth, and a stronger, more authentic sense of self after the significant life change of divorce. Embrace this time as a valuable opportunity to nurture the relationship you have with yourself.

Practical Ways to Befriend Solitude

Learning to embrace solitude after the shared life of a marriage can feel like navigating uncharted territory. It's a process that unfolds gradually, with small steps leading to a greater sense of comfort and even enjoyment in your own company. Be patient and gentle with yourself as you explore these practical ways to befriend this time alone:

- **Start Small:** You don't need to suddenly become a hermit. Begin by incorporating short, intentional moments of solitude into your day.
  - **Sit with your coffee undistracted for 5 minutes.** Instead of immediately turning on the television or reaching for your phone, take a few moments to simply sit with your morning coffee or tea. Notice the warmth of the mug, the aroma, the quiet of the morning. This brief, undistracted time can be a gentle way to ease into your own thoughts and presence. *Aha moment: Realizing that even short, intentional moments of being alone can offer a sense of calm and connection with yourself.*
  - **Take a walk without headphones.** Leave the distractions behind and allow yourself to simply be present with your surroundings. Notice the sights, sounds, and smells around you. Let your thoughts wander without judgment. This can be a refreshing way to connect with your inner world and observe the beauty of the world around you. *Aha moment: Discovering the value of engaging with your own thoughts and the world around you without the filter of external noise.*
  - **Cook one meal just for you, with care.** Instead of throwing something together quickly, take the time to prepare a meal that you truly enjoy. Savor the process of cooking and then sit down to eat it mindfully,

appreciating the nourishment you are giving yourself. This simple act of self-care can foster a sense of appreciation for your own company. *Aha moment: Understanding how nurturing yourself through simple acts like cooking can make solitude feel more comforting and enjoyable.*

- **Create Rituals:** Establishing regular routines around your alone time can help to make it feel more intentional and less like an absence of something else.
  - o **A weekly "date with yourself."** Dedicate a specific time each week to do something you enjoy on your own. This could be visiting a museum, browsing a bookstore, going for a hike, or simply treating yourself to a quiet evening at home with a good book. By scheduling this time and treating it as you would a date with a friend, you are signaling its importance. *Aha moment: Recognizing the benefit of intentionally scheduling and valuing time alone for personal enjoyment and self-discovery.*
  - o **Morning pages.** Make it a habit to write three pages of stream-of-consciousness journaling first thing in the morning. Don't worry about grammar or making sense; just let your thoughts flow onto the page. This practice can be a powerful way to clear your mind, process emotions, and connect with your inner voice in the quiet of solitude. *Aha moment: Discovering how journaling in solitude can facilitate self-expression,*

emotional release, and a deeper understanding of your thoughts and feelings.

- o **A bedtime gratitude reflection.** Before you go to sleep, take a few moments to think about the things you are grateful for. This practice can help to end your day on a positive note and foster a sense of peace and contentment in your own company as you drift off to sleep. *Aha moment: Seeing the value of ending the day with positive reflection during your alone time, cultivating a sense of gratitude and peace.*

- **Reframe the Narrative:** The language you use to describe your alone time can significantly impact how you experience it. Try consciously replacing negative self-talk with more positive and empowering affirmations.
  - o Instead of thinking, "I'm alone," try saying to yourself: **"I'm in conversation with myself."** This reframe emphasizes the opportunity for self-reflection and inner dialogue that solitude provides. *Aha moment: Realizing that being alone can be a valuable time for self-reflection and gaining insights.*
  - o Replace "I have no one to spend time with" with: **"I'm giving myself the attention I deserve."** This shifts the focus from a perceived lack to an act of self-care and validation. *Aha moment: Understanding that choosing to spend time alone can be an*

act of self-love and prioritizing your own well-being.

    o   Instead of "I'm just by myself again," try: **"I'm building a relationship with my future."** This reframe highlights the opportunity for personal growth and self-discovery that solitude offers as you create your new chapter. ***Aha moment:*** *Recognizing that time alone can be a valuable investment in your personal growth and the future you are building.*

Befriending solitude is a journey of self-discovery and growth. By taking small, consistent steps and reframing your perspective, you can transform this time into a valuable and enriching part of your life after divorce.

When Solitude Feels Like Too Much

Navigating the Hard Moments (If loneliness surges):

When those familiar pangs of loneliness arise, despite your efforts to embrace solitude, here are some gentle strategies you can try:

- **Name it: "This is loneliness, not truth."** Simply acknowledging the feeling for what it is can sometimes lessen its power. Remind yourself that loneliness is a temporary emotion, not a reflection of your worth or your future. It's a feeling passing through you, not a permanent state of being. ***Aha moment:*** *Recognizing that naming the emotion* *can help you detach from it and understand it as a temporary feeling rather than an absolute truth.*

- **Reach out: Text a friend "Thinking of you."** You don't need to launch into a deep conversation or explain your feelings in detail. A simple message letting someone know you're thinking of them can be a gentle way to bridge the gap and feel a connection without overwhelming yourself. You might be surprised by the warmth and support you receive in return. *Aha moment: Understanding that reaching out for connection can be as simple as a brief message and can offer a sense of being seen and remembered.*

- **Move through it: Stretch, shower, or step outside.** Sometimes, shifting your physical state can help to shift your emotional state. Engage in some gentle stretching, take a refreshing shower, or simply step outside for some fresh air and sunlight. A change of scenery or physical activity can help to disrupt the cycle of lonely thoughts and bring you back to the present moment. *Aha moment: Recognizing the powerful connection between your physical and emotional well-being and using simple physical actions to navigate feelings of loneliness.*

When to Seek Connection (Solitude becomes unhealthy when):

It's important to be aware of the signs that your alone time might be veering into unhealthy isolation. Here are some indicators to watch out for:

- **You isolate out of self-punishment.** Suppose you find yourself avoiding connection with others because you feel you don't deserve it or as a way to punish yourself for the divorce or perceived failures; this is a sign that your solitude has become unhealthy. Intentional solitude is about self-care and reflection; isolation driven by negativity is not. *Aha moment: Recognizing the difference between choosing solitude for positive reasons and using isolation as a form of self-criticism or punishment.*

- **Weeks pass without meaningful contact.** While everyone's social needs differ, if you realize that weeks are going by without any genuine connection or meaningful interaction with others, this can be detrimental to your well-being. Human connection is vital for our emotional health, and prolonged isolation can lead to increased feelings of loneliness and depression. *Aha moment: Understanding the fundamental human need for connection and recognizing when your level of social interaction is becoming too limited.*

- **Negative thoughts spiral uncontrollably.** Solitude can be a time for reflection, but if you find yourself trapped in a cycle of relentless negative thoughts that you can't break free from, and there's no one to offer a different perspective or support, this is a sign that you might need to reach out. Unchecked negative thinking can be very damaging to your mental health. *Aha moment: Recognizing the link between prolonged isolation and the escalation of negative thought patterns and the importance of seeking external support to break those cycles.*

Remember, seeking connection when you need it is not a sign of weakness; it's an act of self-love and self-awareness. If you find yourself consistently experiencing the signs above, reaching out to a trusted friend, family member, or therapist can provide the support and connection you need to navigate these challenging moments and find a healthier balance between solitude and connection. You are not meant to go through this entirely alone.

The Ultimate Relationship; Falling in Love with Yourself

In the journey of healing and rediscovery after divorce, you might find yourself focusing on mending relationships with friends and family or perhaps even considering new romantic connections. While these external relationships are valuable, there is one relationship that underpins all others and deserves your utmost attention and care: the relationship you have with yourself. This is the ultimate, most enduring bond you will ever have, and nurturing it is a profound act of self-love that can bring immense peace and strength.

Here are some **Questions to Deepen Self-Knowledge** and cultivate a stronger connection with yourself:

- **What makes me feel most alive?** Take some time to ponder this question deeply. What activities, hobbies, or experiences truly ignite your passion and make you feel fully engaged and energized? Perhaps it's spending time in nature, creating something with your hands, learning a new skill, or connecting with others in a meaningful way. Identifying what makes you feel most alive is key to nurturing your inner spirit and building a life that resonates with your authentic self. *Aha moment: Gain clarity on your* *personal sources of vitality and recognize the importance of incorporating them into your life.*

- **How do I want to be spoken to? (Then, speak to yourself that way.)** Consider the way you would speak to someone you deeply care about – with kindness, understanding, and encouragement. Now, turn that same gentle and compassionate voice inward. Pay attention to your inner dialogue and consciously choose to speak to yourself with the same love and respect you would offer a beloved friend. Replace self-criticism with self-compassion and offer yourself words of encouragement and understanding, especially during challenging moments. ***Aha moment:*** *Recognizing the power of your internal voice and making a conscious choice to cultivate a more loving and supportive inner dialogue.*

- **What boundaries do I need to feel safe and valued?** Think about the limits and guidelines you need to establish in your life – both with yourself and with others – to protect your emotional, physical, and mental well-being. What kind of treatment do you deserve? What kind of energy do you want to surround yourself with? Setting healthy boundaries is not selfish; it's an essential act of self-respect and a way to honor your own worth. ***Aha moment:*** *Understanding the importance of establishing and maintaining clear boundaries as a fundamental act of self-love and self-preservation.*

Consider engaging in this **Self-Marriage Exercise** as a symbolic way to deepen your commitment to yourself:

Write vows to yourself, just as you might in a marriage ceremony. Consider including promises like:

- **"I promise to honor my needs..."** This vow signifies your commitment to prioritizing your well-being, listening to your inner guidance, and ensuring your needs are met. It's about recognizing that your own care is paramount.
- **"...to forgive my mistakes..."** This acknowledges that you are human and will inevitably make errors along the way. It's a promise to extend yourself grace and understanding, learning from your mistakes without dwelling in self-blame.
- **"...and to show up for myself as I would a beloved partner."** This is the heart of self-love – treating yourself with the same care, compassion, support, and understanding that you would offer to someone you deeply cherish. It's about being your own best advocate and unwavering supporter.

You can personalize these vows to reflect your own unique needs and aspirations. **Aha moment:** Experiencing a deeper sense of commitment and love towards yourself through the intentional act of writing and reflecting on these personal vows.

Cultivating a loving and supportive relationship with yourself is a journey, not a destination. Be patient and kind to yourself as you embark on this profound and transformative path. This is the ultimate relationship, the one that will be with you throughout your entire life, and nurturing it with love and care is the greatest gift you can give yourself.

Closing: The Return to Yourself

Solitude, dear reader, is often misunderstood. It's not simply the absence of others, a void left behind by the ending of a relationship. In its truest form, especially in the context of healing after divorce, solitude is not the absence of love. It is love's quietest, most enduring form, the love you cultivate for yourself when there's no one else to perform for, no one else to please. It's in these moments of quiet reflection and self-awareness that you have the precious opportunity to nurture the most important relationship you will ever have – the one with yourself.

Some days, this embrace of solitude will feel like a gentle meditation, a peaceful communion with your own thoughts and feelings. You might find a sense of calm and clarity washing over you as you simply allow yourself to be present in your own company. These moments can be deeply restorative, offering a sanctuary where you can recharge and reconnect with your inner wisdom.

On other days, however, your time in solitude might feel more like a wrestling match. You might grapple with difficult emotions, confront uncomfortable truths, or navigate moments of intense self-reflection that can be challenging. Please know that both of these experiences are valid and valuable. Just like the ebb and flow of a dance, there will be moments of grace and moments of struggle.

Here are some key understandings to carry with you about solitude:

- **Solitude is not the same as loneliness.** While loneliness can be a painful feeling of isolation, solitude is a chosen or embraced state of being alone that offers opportunities for self-discovery and peace.

- **Solitude is a powerful pathway to self-love.** By intentionally spending time with yourself, you are demonstrating that you value your own company, your own thoughts, and your own well-being.
- **Solitude can bring both peace and challenge.** It's a space where you can find tranquility but also a space where you might confront difficult emotions that require your attention and compassion.
- **Ultimately, solitude is a return to yourself.** It's an opportunity to peel back the layers of external expectations and reconnect with the core of who you are, independent of any partnership.

Here, in the stillness of your own company, you are not truly alone. You are in the presence of someone extraordinary: the person who has been waiting to be rediscovered all along. Embrace this time, be patient with yourself, and allow the quiet of solitude to guide you on your journey back to the beautiful, resilient, and unique individual that you are.

Reflection Questions: A Path to Self-Understanding

These reflection questions are gentle invitations to acknowledge the progress you've made in befriending solitude and to appreciate the unique comfort that can be found in your own company. Take a few quiet moments with each of these, allowing your honest thoughts and feelings to surface without judgment. There are no right or wrong answers, only opportunities for deeper self-understanding and a greater appreciation for your own presence.

What's one thing I've enjoyed doing alone that surprised me? Think back over the past weeks or months, those moments when you found yourself with your own company. Has there been an activity you engaged in by yourself that you found surprisingly enjoyable, perhaps even more so than you anticipated? Maybe it was lingering over a cup of coffee with a captivating book, taking a leisurely and unplanned walk in nature, losing yourself in a creative pursuit, or simply savoring the quiet of your own home without feeling restless or lonely. Recalling the specific details of these moments and the emotions they evoked can highlight your growing comfort in solitude and reveal unexpected pleasures in your own company, demonstrating a positive shift in your relationship with yourself. It's a wonderful way to acknowledge the subtle yet significant positive shifts that are taking place within you. Aha moment: Realizing your capacity for enjoyment and contentment in your own company, perhaps in ways you hadn't expected, can foster a deeper sense of self-acceptance and peace.

How has solitude served me in the past? Reflect on specific instances throughout your life, both before and after your divorce, where your time alone has been beneficial or restorative. Perhaps solitude provided you with the necessary space to process difficult emotions without external pressures, allowed you to gain clarity on a challenging situation by listening to your own inner voice, enabled you to tap into your creativity without distraction, or simply offered a chance to recharge and rejuvenate your energy levels. Recognizing the tangible ways in which solitude has served you in the past can help you to appreciate its inherent value and to approach future moments of being alone with a greater sense of openness and anticipation for the potential benefits and insights it might hold for your well-being. Aha moment: Identifying specific positive outcomes from past experiences of solitude can build trust in its current and future value for your healing and growth.

If my future self thanked me for this solitary time, what would they say? Imagine yourself a year or even several years from now, looking back at this particular period of your life, this time of intentional or circumstantial solitude. If that future version of you, having experienced the benefits of this time, were to express gratitude for the moments you are now spending in your own company, what might they be thankful for? Perhaps they would acknowledge the profound self-discovery you embarked on, the inner strength you cultivated in your quiet moments, the deeper understanding you gained of your own needs and desires, or the more authentic and loving relationship you built with yourself. This question encourages you to consider the long-term, positive impact of embracing solitude and to see this time not as an empty void but as a valuable investment in your future well-being, happiness, and personal growth. Aha moment: Envisioning your future self and expressing gratitude for your present embrace of solitude can provide a powerful sense of purpose and validation of the value of this time.

Chapter 11:
Venturing into the World Again

The Courage to Re-Engage

In the delicate process of healing after divorce, there often comes a time when the solitude you've intentionally cultivated, the walls you've built around yourself for protection and solace, begin to feel different. What once offered a much-needed sanctuary, a safe haven to process your emotions and reconnect with yourself, might start to feel less like a comforting embrace and more like a restrictive cage. The world outside, once a familiar landscape, can now appear foreign and perhaps even a little intimidating.

You might find yourself looking out at that world, feeling a pull to re-engage, but also experiencing a wave of anxieties:

- Will I still fit in? You might wonder if your place in your social circles has shifted or if you still share common ground with those you once felt close to.
- Do I remember how to be "me" out there? After a period of focusing inward, you might feel uncertain about how to present yourself in social situations, unsure of who "you" are now in this new context.
- What if I get hurt again? The vulnerability of opening yourself up to the world after experiencing the pain of divorce can be a significant barrier, and the fear of further heartache is entirely understandable.

Please know that these fears are not only valid but also incredibly natural. After the seismic shift of divorce, even seemingly simple social interactions can feel like navigating uncharted territory. It's as if the rules have changed, and you're unsure of the new landscape. But here's a gentle truth that your heart needs to hear and hold onto: The world has missed you. And the version of you that is emerging from this experience, wiser, more authentic, and undeniably resilient, has so much to offer it.

This chapter isn't about pushing you to rush back into the thick of things before you're ready, nor is it about pretending that those fears don't exist. It's about honoring your hesitation, acknowledging the understandable desire to protect yourself while also gently encouraging you to stretch beyond those self-imposed walls, one small, brave step at a time. It's about recognizing that re-engagement is a courageous act and that every tentative step you take back into the world is a victory in itself.

The Emotional Landscape of Re-Entry

Stepping back into the world after the significant life shift of divorce can feel like navigating a landscape dotted with familiar landmarks that now appear slightly different. Social situations that once felt comfortable and routine might now evoke a mix of complex and sometimes daunting emotions. It's important to acknowledge and normalize these feelings, understanding that they are a natural response to such a profound change.

Here's why venturing out socially might feel so challenging post-divorce:

- Identity uncertainty (Who am I in groups now?) For a long time, your social identity might have been intertwined with your role as part of a couple. Now, as a single individual, you might feel a sense of uncertainty about how you fit into existing social dynamics. You might wonder how to introduce yourself, how to navigate conversations about your relationship status, or even if you still share the same common ground with friends who knew you primarily as part of a "we." This feeling of not quite knowing your place or how to present yourself is a common experience as you redefine your identity within your social circles. Aha moment: Recognizing that your identity within social groups might feel different now is a natural consequence of your changed circumstances, and it's okay to take time to redefine your place.

- Comparison traps (Everyone else seems so put together) When you're feeling vulnerable or in transition, it's easy to fall into the trap of comparing your inner experience with the outward appearances of others. You might attend social gatherings and perceive that everyone else seems happy, settled, and effortlessly navigating their relationships. It's important to remember that social media and outward presentations often don't reflect the full complexity of people's lives. Everyone has their own struggles and challenges, even if they aren't always visible. Try to focus on your own journey and celebrate your own progress rather than getting caught in the comparison game. Aha moment: Understanding that outward appearances can be deceiving and focusing on your own healing and growth is more important than comparing yourself to others.

- Vulnerability hangovers (Was I too much? Not enough?) After putting yourself out there and engaging in social interactions, you might experience what some call a "vulnerability hangover." This involves overthinking your interactions, questioning whether you shared too much or too little, or feeling self-conscious about how you came across. This feeling of emotional exposure is common, especially when you're still navigating your comfort level by sharing your personal experiences. Be kind to yourself, and remember that genuine connection often involves some degree of vulnerability. Aha moment: Realizing that feeling emotionally exposed or self-critical after socializing is a common reaction during this time, and practicing self-compassion is key.

Normalize This: Of course, it feels strange to re-enter the social world. You're not simply returning to the person you were before your divorce; you're arriving as someone new, someone who has been through a significant transformation. Allow yourself the grace to feel a little awkward or uncertain as you find your footing.

The Re-Entry Spectrum

Think of your comfort level with social re-entry as a spectrum:

- **Comfortable:** Activities that feel safe and easy, like texting a close friend or spending time in your own home.
- **Stretch:** Activities that push you slightly outside your comfort zone but feel manageable, like having lunch one-on-one with a friend or attending a small gathering.
- **Panic Zone:** Activities that feel overwhelming and trigger significant anxiety, like attending a large party or a crowded event before you feel ready.

Strategy: Aim to spend most of your time in the "Stretch" zone. This allows you to gently challenge yourself and grow without becoming overwhelmed. It's about finding that sweet spot of just enough discomfort to encourage progress but not so much that it triggers significant anxiety or a desire to retreat completely. Be patient with yourself and honor your own pace as you navigate this emotional landscape of re-entry.

The Re-Entry Spectrum

Think of your journey back into the social world as a gradual expansion of your comfort zone. It's helpful to visualize this as a spectrum with different levels of ease and challenge:

- **Comfortable Zone:** These are the activities that feel safe and require little emotional energy. This might include texting a close friend, having a quiet conversation with a family member, or spending time in familiar, low-pressure environments. These activities provide a gentle foundation as you begin to re-engage.
- **Stretch Zone:** This is where the real growth happens. These are the activities that push you slightly outside your comfort zone but still feel manageable. Perhaps it's meeting a friend for a one-on-one lunch, attending a small gathering where you know a few people, or trying a new, low-stakes activity in a group setting. This zone offers just enough discomfort to encourage growth without overwhelming you.
- **Panic Zone:** These are the situations that feel overwhelming and trigger significant anxiety. Attending a large, crowded party or forcing yourself into intense social interactions before you feel ready

can land you in this zone. While pushing your boundaries is important, it's also crucial to avoid situations that feel truly panic-inducing, as this can lead to setbacks.

The key strategy here is to spend most of your time in the Stretch Zone. This allows you to gently challenge yourself, build confidence, and gradually expand your comfort level without feeling overwhelmed or retreating completely. Pay attention to how different situations make you feel, honor your own pace, and remember that it's okay to take small, brave steps forward.

Reconnecting With Your People

Navigating friendships after divorce can feel like a delicate dance. Some relationships will naturally shift, while others might surprise you with their depth and resilience. Remember that your connections with others are a vital source of support and joy as you navigate this new chapter.

Navigating Friendships Post-Divorce (With Old Friends)

- **Some will surprise you with depth:** You might find that certain friendships you had before or during your marriage blossom into even more meaningful connections now. Perhaps these friends always sensed your underlying needs or have a deep understanding of your core self. They might offer unwavering support, a listening ear without judgment, and a level of empathy that truly comforts you. Cherish these friendships; they are anchors in your journey. *Aha moment: Recognizing the unexpected strength and depth of some existing friendships can be a beautiful and reassuring discovery.*

- **Others may drift, but this hurts, and it isn't a failure.** It's also a reality that some friendships might naturally evolve or drift apart after your divorce. This can be painful, especially if these are long-standing connections. Try to remember that this isn't necessarily a reflection of your worth or a failure on your part. Sometimes, shared connections through your former partner might have been the primary bond, or perhaps your life paths are simply diverging. Allow yourself to grieve these shifts, but also make space for new connections that align with who you are becoming now. *Aha moment: Understanding that some friendships might naturally evolve after divorce is a normal part of life's changes and not necessarily a personal failing.*

- **Try: "I'm rediscovering myself. Do you want to try something new together?"** This simple invitation can be a wonderful way to reconnect with old friends in the context of your evolving identity. Suggest an activity you've always wanted to try or something that reflects a new interest. This shows your friends that you value their company and are open to new experiences together, creating fresh shared memories beyond the framework of your marriage. Examples could be trying a new restaurant, going to a concert, taking a hike, or attending a workshop. *Aha moment: Seeing proactive ways* *to revitalize existing friendships by inviting friends to join you in exploring new aspects of your life.*

Making new friends

Divorce can also create an opportunity to expand your social circle and connect with people who share your current interests and passions.

- **Join groups aligned with current interests (meetup.com, classes):** Think about the hobbies or activities that bring you joy. Joining a local hiking group, a book club, a painting class, or a volunteer organization is a fantastic way to meet people who share common ground with you. These connections often form organically around a shared focus, making it easier to build rapport. ***Aha moment:*** *Realizing that pursuing your interests is a natural way to meet like-minded individuals and forge new friendships.*
- **Lead with curiosity: "What's your story?" disarms more than small talk.** When meeting new people, try shifting the focus from surface-level small talk to genuine curiosity about their lives and experiences. Asking open-ended questions like "What are you passionate about?" or "What brought you here today?" can lead to more meaningful conversations and create a deeper connection than discussing the weather. ***Aha moment:*** *Understanding the power of genuine curiosity in initiating more meaningful connections and building new friendships.*

Script for Awkward Moments

Navigating social situations where your divorce might come up can sometimes feel awkward. Here's a helpful script you can adapt:

- **"I'm still getting used to talking about myself as 'I' instead of 'we.' Bear with me!"** This is a lighthearted and honest way to address any potential fumbles or moments of adjustment as you redefine your social narrative. It acknowledges the change without dwelling on the details and invites understanding from others.

Remember, building and maintaining friendships takes time and effort. Be patient with yourself and with others as you navigate these evolving connections. Both your old friends and the new connections you make will enrich your life in unique and valuable ways.

The Joy of Rediscovering Play

After navigating the often serious and emotionally taxing terrain of divorce, it's essential to remember the importance of joy, lightness, and simply having fun. Rediscovering play through hobbies and enjoyable activities can be a powerful antidote to stress and a wonderful way to nurture your well-being as you rebuild your life. Engaging in activities purely for the pleasure they bring can rewire your brain, reconnect you with your authentic self, and create opportunities for new connections.

Why Hobbies Matter Now

- **Rewire your brain beyond grief pathways:**
When you're processing significant loss, it's easy for
your thoughts to become stuck in patterns of grief
and rumination. Engaging in new and enjoyable
activities can help to create new neural pathways in
your brain, shifting your focus and energy towards
something positive and engaging. This can provide a
much-needed break from difficult emotions and
help you to experience moments of genuine joy. *Aha
moment: Understanding that engaging in new
activities can have a tangible, positive impact on
your brain, helping you to move beyond patterns of
grief.*

- **Reveal parts of yourself buried in the
marriage:** Over the course of a relationship, you
might have put certain interests or passions on hold.
Now is the perfect time to reconnect with those
buried parts of yourself or to discover entirely new
ones. Perhaps you used to love painting, playing a
sport, or learning about astronomy. Or maybe you've
always been curious about pottery, creative writing,
or volunteering. Exploring these avenues can reveal
aspects of your identity that might have been
dormant, bringing a renewed sense of self-discovery
and fulfillment. *Aha moment: Realizing that
hobbies can be a direct pathway to rediscovering
forgotten passions or uncovering entirely new
facets of your identity.*

- **Create natural social connections:** Engaging in
hobbies, especially in group settings, provides a
relaxed and organic way to connect with others who
share similar interests. This can be a much less

pressure-filled way to socialize than traditional "networking" or dating. Whether it's joining a book club, a hiking group, a cooking class, or a volunteer organization, shared activities create a natural foundation for building new friendships and a sense of community. ***Aha moment:*** *Seeing hobbies as a fun and low-pressure way to build new social connections based on genuine shared interests.*

Ideas to Spark Inspiration

Here are some ideas to get you started, categorized by commitment level and social interaction:

- **Low Commitment:**
  - Adult coloring books
  - Listening to podcasts on intriguing topics
  - Trying out different types of tea or coffee
  - Learning a few phrases in a new language
  - Exploring free online courses

- **Social:**
  - Dance classes (salsa, swing, ballroom)
  - Joining a recreational sports team
  - Volunteering for a cause you care about
  - Attending local workshops or lectures
  - Joining a book club or a movie group

- **Solo:**
  - Photography walks in your neighborhood.
  - Learning to play a musical instrument
  - Creative writing or journaling
  - Gardening or tending to houseplants

o   Exploring different forms of art (painting, drawing, sculpting)

Mantra: As you explore these new or rediscovered activities, remember this gentle mantra: "I don't have to be good , just curious." Release any pressure to be perfect or to achieve a certain level of skill. The goal here is simply to engage with curiosity, to have fun, and to allow yourself the freedom to explore without judgment. Aha moment: Feeling liberated from the expectation of mastery and embracing the simple joy of exploration and curiosity.

Allow yourself the gift of play. Embrace the opportunity to rediscover what brings you joy, to connect with others through shared interests, and to nurture your well-being through engaging and enjoyable activities. This is a time for exploration and self-discovery, so be open to trying new things and remember that the most important thing is to have fun along the way.

Dating Again (If and When You're Ready)

The decision to start dating again after divorce is a deeply personal one, with no right or wrong timeline. Some might feel a pull to explore new connections relatively soon, while others may need more time for healing and self-discovery. Wherever you are on this spectrum is perfectly valid. This section is here to offer some gentle guidance if and when the idea of dating begins to feel like something you might want to consider.

Signs You Might Be Ready

The readiness to date again isn't about meeting a specific milestone; it's more about an internal shift in your emotional landscape. Here are some signs that you might be approaching that point:

- **You can think of your ex without intense emotion:** When memories of your former partner surface, do they primarily evoke a sense of neutrality or perhaps a gentle sadness rather than intense anger, bitterness, or longing? This emotional detachment suggests that you've processed some of the core pain and are not primarily looking to replace what was lost. *Aha moment: Recognizing that you can reflect on your past relationship without being overwhelmed by intense negative emotions can be a clear sign of emotional readiness to move forward.*

- **You're dating to add to your life, not fill it:** Are you considering dating as a way to enhance an already fulfilling life, or are you hoping it will fill a void or provide a sense of completeness? Entering the dating world from a place of wholeness rather than neediness is a much healthier approach. It indicates that you've cultivated a strong sense of self and are looking for a connection to enhance your happiness, not to define it. *Aha moment: Understanding that dating should be about adding value to your life rather than trying to find someone to "fix" your feelings or make you whole.*

- **The idea excites more than terrifies you (51% vs 49% is enough!):** It's perfectly normal to feel a mix of excitement and apprehension when considering dating again, especially after a significant relationship ends. However, if the feeling of excitement outweighs the fear, even by a small margin, that can be a good indicator that you're leaning in the right direction. You don't need to be completely fearless; a slight pull towards the possibility of connection is often enough to take those first steps. *Aha moment: Reassuring yourself that you don't need to be completely free of fear to start dating; a slight sense of excitement and curiosity is a positive sign.*

Baby Steps Back In

If you're feeling those initial nudges of readiness, there's no need to dive headfirst into the deep end. Here are some gentle baby steps you can take:

- **Flirt with the idea first:** Simply allow yourself to notice attractive people or feel a spark of connection without any pressure to act on it. This is about getting comfortable with the idea of attraction and possibility again.
- **Try a "practice date" with someone low-stakes:** Consider connecting with someone you find interesting but don't feel intense pressure to impress. This could be someone you meet through a hobby or a casual acquaintance. The goal is to ease back into the rhythm of conversation and connection in a dating context without high expectations.
- **Set boundaries early: "I'm taking things slow, just FYI!"** Be open and honest about your intentions and your pace. Communicating early on that you're taking things slow can help to manage expectations and ensure you feel comfortable.

Red Flags vs. Green Flags:

As you navigate the dating world, it's helpful to be aware of potential red and green flags:

Red Flags	Green Flags
Pressures you to "get over" your past quickly	Respects your healing timeline and acknowledges your journey
Talks badly about all their exes	Shows self-awareness about their past relationships
Seems overly critical or judgmental	Is kind, empathetic, and a good listener
Rushes intimacy or commitment	Allows things to unfold naturally and at a comfortable pace
Doesn't respect your boundaries	Honors and respects your boundaries

Remember, your peace and well-being are paramount. A "no" that honors your peace is always better than a "yes" that betrays it. Trust your instincts, be kind to yourself, and enjoy the process of exploring new connections when you feel genuinely ready.

When the World Feels Overwhelming

Even when your ventures back into the world are positive and enjoyable, you might find that socializing can sometimes leave you feeling unexpectedly drained. Think of it like a "social hangover", that feeling of being emotionally or mentally fatigued after a period of engagement, even if the interactions themselves were pleasant. This is a perfectly normal response as you navigate re-entry after divorce. It takes energy to be present, to connect, and to navigate new or altered social dynamics.

Here's what that "Social Hangover" might feel like and some ways to care for yourself afterward:

- After socializing, you might feel:
    - **Drained (even if it went well):** Even positive social interactions require energy. You might find yourself feeling physically or emotionally tired, even if you genuinely enjoyed the company and the event. This is simply a sign that you've exerted energy in connecting with others. *Aha moment: Understanding that feeling tired after socializing is a normal and valid response, even if the experience was positive.*
    - **Self-critical (Did I talk too much?):** It's common to overanalyze your social interactions afterward, wondering if you said the right things, shared too much or came across in the way you intended. Try to be kind to yourself and remember that most people are focused on their own experiences rather than closely scrutinizing yours. *Aha*

moment: Recognizing that self-criticism after socializing is a common tendency and often not based on reality.

- o **Nostalgic for isolation:** After being around others, you might find yourself craving the quiet and solitude you've come to appreciate during your healing process. This doesn't mean you didn't enjoy socializing; it simply reflects your need for balance and the comfort you find in your own company. *Aha moment:* Understanding that craving alone time after socializing is a natural and healthy need for introverted moments of recharge.

- **Care Plan:** When you experience this "social hangover," be gentle with yourself and try these self-care strategies:
  - o **Hydrate + snack (low blood sugar exacerbates emotion):** Socializing can sometimes disrupt your regular eating and drinking patterns. Low blood sugar or dehydration can amplify feelings of fatigue and emotional sensitivity. Replenishing your body with water and a nutritious snack can make a significant difference in how you feel.
  - o **Shower to "wash off" the energy:** Some people find a shower or bath to be a helpful way to symbolically and physically cleanse themselves of the energy of social interaction. The water can feel soothing and help you to transition back into your own space.
  - o **Journal: "What actually went better than I'm giving myself credit for?"**

Counteract any tendencies towards self-criticism by focusing on the positive aspects of your social interaction. What did you enjoy? What connections did you make? What did you handle well? Shifting your focus to the positives can help to reframe your experience. *Aha moment: Gaining practical, actionable strategies for managing the emotional and physical after-effects of socializing, empowering you to care for yourself.*

- **Permission to Pause:** It's crucial to honor your own limits and give yourself permission to step back when the world feels overwhelming:
    - **Leave early ("I've hit my social limit, thanks for tonight!")**: There's no obligation to stay at a social event until the very end. If you feel your energy waning, it's perfectly acceptable to politely excuse yourself and leave when you need to.
    - **Take a month off dating apps:** If the online dating world starts to feel draining or stressful, give yourself permission to take a break. You can always return to it when you feel more refreshed.
    - **Say no to events that drain more than nourish:** You don't have to accept every invitation you receive. Be selective about how you spend your social energy and prioritize events that genuinely bring you joy and connection rather than those that leave you feeling depleted. *Aha moment: Recognizing and honoring your own social*

limits is an act of self-care and allows you to engage with the world in a way that feels sustainable for you.

Remember, navigating re-entry is a process, and it's okay to have days when you need to retreat and recharge. Be kind and patient with yourself as you find your own rhythm.

Celebrating Your Brave Steps

Okay, let's expand on the "Celebrating Your Brave Steps" section from Chapter 11.

The journey of venturing back into the world after divorce is paved with small acts of courage, micro-milestones that might seem insignificant on their own but collectively represent tremendous progress. It's so important to acknowledge and celebrate these brave steps you're taking. This isn't about grand gestures or overnight transformations; it's about recognizing the quiet strength you're demonstrating in your everyday efforts to re-engage with life.

Micro-Milestones Matter

Think about some of the seemingly small things you've done recently. Did you...

- **Initiate a text to a friend you haven't spoken to in a while?** That simple act of reaching out takes vulnerability and a willingness to reconnect. It shows you're putting yourself out there and nurturing your relationships. ***Aha moment:***

Recognizing the bravery in initiating a connection, even though a simple text message.

- **Go to a café alone for the first time?** Stepping into a public space on your own can feel daunting initially. This act demonstrates your growing comfort in your own company and your willingness to experience life independently. ***Aha moment:*** *Acknowledging the strength in enjoying your own presence in a social setting.*

- **Wear an outfit that truly feels like "you," even if it's a little outside your old comfort zone?** Expressing your authentic self through your appearance is a sign of your evolving identity and a courageous step towards embracing who you are now. ***Aha moment:*** *Seeing the significance of aligning your outward presentation with your inner sense of self.*

But the list doesn't stop there. Consider if you have also...

- Said "yes" to a social invitation, even if you felt a little nervous?
- Had a conversation with a new person you met?
- Tried a new activity or visited a new place on your own?
- Shared a small part of your experience with someone you trust?
- Set a boundary that felt right for you, even if it was difficult?

These are all victories. Each small step you take, each time you push yourself just a little bit beyond your comfort zone, is a testament to your resilience and your courage in navigating this new chapter. Don't underestimate the power of these seemingly minor actions. They are the building blocks of your re-engagement with the world.

Ritual: Light a candle weekly to honor your courage

Consider creating a simple weekly ritual to acknowledge your bravery. Perhaps light a candle each week and take a few moments to reflect on the brave steps you've taken, big or small. This can be a dedicated time for self-acknowledgement and celebration of your progress. Aha moment: Understanding the value of creating a consistent ritual to honor your courage and reinforce your positive steps forward.

Remember, this journey isn't always linear. There might be days when you feel more courageous than others, and that's perfectly okay. Be patient and compassionate with yourself. Every step forward, no matter how small it seems, is a victory worth celebrating. You are showing up for yourself, and that is the bravest thing you can do.

Closing: The World Needs the You You're Becoming

Every time you gather the courage to step back into the world, whether it's a small outing for coffee with a friend or simply sitting in a park surrounded by the rhythm of life, you are doing something truly significant. You are showing up not as the person you were before this journey but as the evolved, resilient individual you are becoming. And please know this: the world needs the you you're becoming. Your unique experiences, your newfound wisdom, and your authentic self-have something valuable to offer.

Remember these important points as you continue to venture out:

- **Showing Up is Sacred Work:** Each time you choose to engage with the world, even in small ways, you are proving to yourself that joy and connection are still within your reach and that you are worthy of experiencing them. This act of showing up is a testament to your strength and your commitment to healing.

- **Embrace the Ups and Downs:** Some days, re-engaging will feel awkward, perhaps even a little painful. There might be moments of uncertainty or discomfort. But other days will surprise you with their sweetness – the unexpected laughter shared with a friend, the kindness of a stranger that feels like a gift, or the simple joy of feeling connected to the world around you.

- **You Are Still Here:** The realization that "I'm still here" and "It's good to be back" is a powerful one. It signifies a return to a sense of belonging, a reconnection with the vibrant tapestry of life. Embrace this feeling of being present and engaged in the world once more.

Your journey of re-engagement is a testament to your resilience and your unwavering spirit. Every step you take, no matter how small, is a brave act. Trust in the person you are becoming, and know that your presence in the world is valuable and needed. Embrace the opportunities for connection and joy that await you, one courageous step at a time.

Reflection Questions: A Path to Self-Understanding

These reflection questions are designed to help you acknowledge the brave steps you've already taken towards re-engaging with the world and tap into the inner courage that will continue to guide you forward. Take a few quiet moments with each of these, allowing your honest thoughts and feelings to surface without judgment. There are no right or wrong answers, only opportunities for deeper self-awareness and a greater appreciation for your own resilience.

What's one tiny way I've already begun re-engaging? Think back over the past week or two, or even further if it feels right. What is one small step you've taken to venture back into the world, no matter how seemingly insignificant it might feel? Did you send a simple text message to an old friend? Did you strike up a brief conversation with a cashier at the grocery store? Did you visit a familiar café on your own for a few minutes? Recognizing these initial efforts, these tiny acts of courage that might have felt a little daunting at the time are so important. It validates your progress and serves as a tangible reminder that you are already on your way, even if it doesn't always feel like a monumental leap forward. Acknowledging these small victories can build valuable momentum and gently encourage you to take the next brave step on your path. Aha moment: Realizing that you have already demonstrated courage in re-engaging, even in small ways, can boost your confidence and encourage further steps forward.

What's a social setting I used to enjoy that I might try again? Consider social activities or environments that you genuinely enjoyed in the past, perhaps before or even during your marriage, where you felt a sense of comfort or connection. Is there a book club you were once a part of? A favorite coffee shop where you always felt comfortable and welcomed? A type of community event or gathering you used to look forward to attending? Thinking about these familiar and positive experiences can offer a gentle and less intimidating starting point for re-engaging with the social world. There's absolutely no pressure to jump back into everything at once, but simply considering these possibilities can open doors to reconnecting with activities and people you once found joy and comfort in, potentially easing the feeling of the unknown. Aha moment: Identifying a previously enjoyed social setting can provide a sense of familiarity and reduce the anxiety associated with venturing into new or unknown social situations.

If my bravest self had one message for me today, what would it be? Take a moment to connect with that part of you that is inherently courageous, the part that knows you possess the strength to overcome challenges and embrace new experiences, even when they feel a little scary. If that brave and resilient self could whisper one message of guidance or encouragement to you right now, in this very moment, what do you sense it would be? Would it be an affirmation of your inner strength? An encouraging nudge to take just one small step forward? A gentle reminder that you are worthy of joy and meaningful connection? Tuning into this inner source of courage can provide a powerful boost of confidence and remind you of the incredible resilience and bravery you possess within, ready to guide you on your journey. Aha moment: Connecting with your inner "bravest self" can provide a powerful source of personalized encouragement and strength to navigate your re-engagement with the world.

Journal Prompt:

"Right now, venturing out feels like _____, but I'm proud that I _____."

This prompt invites you to acknowledge any feelings of apprehension, discomfort, or nervousness you might be experiencing about re-engaging with the world. It's perfectly okay and completely understandable to feel a mix of emotions, including some fear or uncertainty. But the second part of the prompt encourages you to also consciously recognize and celebrate your bravery. What is one thing, no matter how small it might seem, that you've already done to venture out that you are genuinely proud of? This exercise helps to create a balance between acknowledging your current feelings and honoring the courage you have already demonstrated, reinforcing your progress and building your self-assurance.

Chapter 12:

The Unseen Blessings

The Wisdom That Comes with Time

There often arrives a moment, perhaps months or even years, after the initial storm of divorce has passed when you might find yourself pausing, taking a deep breath, and suddenly realizing something profound and unexpected: you are not simply surviving the aftermath. You are different. You are stronger than you ever imagined. You are more alive in ways you couldn't have possibly foreseen during those darkest days.

What once felt so definitively like an ending, a closing of a significant chapter now begins to reveal itself as a new beginning, a fresh page waiting to be written. The pain that once felt all-consuming, a heavy weight that threatened to pull you under, has, with the passage of time, transformed. It has become the very soil from which new growth has stubbornly and beautifully emerged. And while you likely would never have chosen this particular path and would never have wished for the heartache and upheaval, you cannot deny the subtle yet undeniable gifts that it has unexpectedly bestowed upon you, gifts you might never have discovered or received had your life continued on its previous course.

This final chapter isn't about trying to sugarcoat the past or minimizing the very real hurt you experienced. It's not about pretending that the pain didn't matter or that the journey was easy. Instead, it's a heartfelt invitation to honor the entirety of your experience by consciously recognizing the hidden blessings that have quietly and intricately woven themselves into the fabric of your life. It's about taking a moment to see just how far you've traveled, to acknowledge the incredible strength you've unearthed within yourself, the profound wisdom you've gained, and the unexpected beauty that has blossomed from what once felt like utter wreckage.

Because the truth, the undeniable truth that time often reveals, is this: you are not the person you were before the storm. You have been reshaped, reformed, and in so many significant and meaningful ways that transformation is a gift. It's a testament to your resilience, your courage, and your inherent capacity for growth. This chapter is a celebration of that transformation, an acknowledgement of the unseen blessings that time and your own inner strength have brought forth.

The Alchemy of Pain – How Suffering Transforms Us

It might seem counterintuitive, but often, it is through our deepest wounds that we discover our greatest strengths. The pain of divorce, while undeniably challenging, has a remarkable capacity to act as a catalyst for profound personal transformation. Think of it like the ancient practice of alchemy, where seemingly base metals are subjected to intense processes to reveal their hidden value. Similarly, the intense experience of suffering can refine us, revealing inner resources and strengths we might never have known we possessed.

This isn't just a poetic notion; science actually confirms what artists and philosophers have long understood: adversity has the power to reshape us in significant and often positive ways. Researchers studying post-traumatic growth have found that after navigating hardship, individuals frequently report a range of positive psychological changes. You, dear reader, are likely living proof of this phenomenon. Consider some of the common benefits observed in individuals who have experienced significant challenges:

- **Greater appreciation for life:** Having faced the fragility and potential for loss in life, many individuals report newfound gratitude for the simple things – the beauty of nature, the warmth of connection, and the joy of everyday moments. You might find yourself savoring experiences more fully and appreciating the present in a way you hadn't before.

- **Deeper relationships:** Shared struggles have a unique way of forging stronger bonds between people. You might find that your relationships with friends and family have deepened, becoming more authentic and supportive as you've navigated this challenging time. You might also have formed new connections with individuals who truly understand your experience, creating a powerful sense of community.

- **New possibilities they hadn't considered before:** Divorce can dismantle old structures and expectations, but in doing so, it can also open doors to new paths and opportunities you might never have considered otherwise. This could involve pursuing a long-held dream, exploring a new career, or simply embracing a lifestyle that feels more authentically aligned with your individual needs and desires.

- **Increased personal strength:** Navigating the complexities and emotional turmoil of divorce requires immense inner strength and resilience. You have likely discovered a fortitude within yourself that you didn't know existed. Overcoming these challenges builds a powerful sense of self-efficacy and the knowledge that you can handle difficult situations.

- **Spiritual or existential deepening:** Facing profound life changes can often lead to a re-evaluation of your values, beliefs, and your sense of purpose in the world. This might involve a deepening of your spiritual practices or a new understanding of what truly matters to you on an existential level.

Exercise: The Before & After Portrait

To help you recognize the incredible transformation you've undergone, consider this exercise:

Draw a line down the center of a page, creating two columns.

- On the left side, label it **"Then Me"** and jot down qualities, feelings, and perspectives that describe how you saw yourself during the darkest days of your divorce journey. Think about your emotional state, your beliefs about yourself, and your outlook on the future.
- On the right side, label it **"Now Me"** and list the qualities, feelings, and perspectives you've discovered or cultivated within yourself since that time. Consider your current strengths, your newfound wisdom, and how your perspective has shifted.

Notice: As you look at both columns, what stands out to you? Which version of yourself feels more authentic? Which one demonstrates greater resilience? Which one embodies more compassion, both for yourself and for others?

This simple exercise can offer a powerful visual representation of the incredible alchemy that has taken place within you, revealing the strength and beauty that have emerged from the pain. You are living proof of the transformative power of the human spirit.

The Blessings You Never Saw Coming

Even amidst the pain and upheaval of divorce, there are often unexpected glimmers of light and blessings that emerge from the experience in ways you might never have anticipated. These are the quiet gifts that can only be unwrapped after navigating the storm, revealing a strength and clarity you might not have known you possessed. Let's explore some of these unforeseen blessings:

1. **The Gift of Self-Rediscovery:** When the familiar structure of your marriage dissolves, it can feel disorienting, but it also creates a unique void, a blank space where you have the opportunity to rediscover who you are at your core, independent of your role as a partner.
    a. **Passions you'd forgotten:** You might find yourself drawn back to hobbies or interests you set aside during your marriage, reigniting a spark of joy and reminding you of what truly excites you as an individual. Perhaps you pick up that old paintbrush again, dust off your hiking boots, or finally learn to play that instrument you always admired. *Aha moment: Realizing that the space left by the marriage has allowed you*

to reconnect with passions that make you uniquely you.

b. **Boundaries you now honor:** Through the experience of divorce, you likely gained a clearer understanding of your own needs and limits. You might find yourself more empowered to establish and honor boundaries in your relationships, ensuring your well-being is prioritized in ways it wasn't before. Learning to say "no" when you need to and protecting your energy becomes an act of self-respect. *Aha moment: Recognizing the newfound strength to assert your boundaries and prioritize your own needs.*

c. **A voice you'd silenced:** In some relationships, one partner's voice might inadvertently overshadow the others. Divorce can create the space for you to rediscover your own voice, express your opinions and needs with confidence, and embrace your authentic self without fear of judgment or compromise. *Aha moment: Understanding the freedom and empowerment that comes with finding and using your own voice.*

d. **"I lost a marriage but found myself."** This sentiment often rings true for those who have navigated divorce, highlighting the profound self-discovery that can emerge from the ashes.

2. **The Clarity of What Really Matters:** When life undergoes a significant upheaval, it has a way of

stripping away the superficial and revealing what truly holds value for you.

a. **Who your true allies are:** During challenging times, you often discover who your genuine supporters are , those friends and family members who show up for you unconditionally, offering unwavering love and support. This clarity can deepen your appreciation for these vital connections. *Aha moment: Recognizing the strength and reliability of your true support system.*

b. **How little you need to be happy:** You might realize that happiness isn't necessarily tied to material possessions or societal expectations. Instead, you might find contentment in simple pleasures, meaningful connections, and a sense of inner peace. *Aha moment: Understanding that true happiness often lies in simplicity and genuine connections rather than external factors.*

c. **What you'll never tolerate again:** The experiences of your marriage and its ending likely provided valuable lessons about what you will and will not accept in future relationships and in your life in general. This newfound clarity empowers you to make healthier choices moving forward. *Aha moment: Recognizing the valuable lessons learned about your personal boundaries and what you deserve in future relationships.*

d. **"I no longer confuse comfort for love."** This insight often emerges, highlighting a deeper understanding of the difference between genuine connection and simply settling for familiarity.

3. **The Unexpected Angels:** Often, during difficult times, people appear in our lives in unexpected ways, offering support, guidance, or simply a kind presence when we need it most.

   a. **The coworker who became a confidant:** Someone at work might have offered a listening ear or practical support that went above and beyond.

   b. **The support group stranger who "got it":** Connecting with others who have shared similar experiences can provide a profound sense of validation and understanding.

   c. **The therapist who helped you rebuild:** Professional guidance can be invaluable in navigating the emotional complexities of divorce.

   d. **"Some blessings wear human skin."** These unexpected connections can feel like gifts, reminding you that you are not alone and that kindness and support exist all around you. ***Aha moment:*** *Appreciating the unexpected kindness and support that emerged from unexpected sources during your journey.*

4. The Strength, You Didn't Know You Had: Navigating the emotional, practical, and sometimes legal complexities of divorce requires a level of strength you might not have known you possessed.

a. **You slept through nights that felt endless:** Even when grief felt overwhelming, you found a way to keep going, day after day.

b. **Showed up when you wanted to hide:** You faced difficult situations and interactions, even when your instinct was to retreat.

c. **Chose hope when despair seemed easier:** You held onto the possibility of a better future, even when it felt distant.

d. **"Turns out I'm the hero I was waiting for."** This powerful realization often emerges, highlighting your own incredible resilience and inner strength. *Aha moment: Recognizing your own remarkable strength and resilience in navigating the challenges of divorce.*

These unseen blessings, these unexpected gifts, are testaments to your strength, your resilience, and your capacity for growth. Take a moment to acknowledge them; they are a beautiful part of your journey.

Writing Your Own Redemption Story

The way we frame our experiences and the stories we tell ourselves about our lives holds immense power in shaping our healing and our future. Divorce can easily be cast as a tragedy, a story of failure or loss. But you have the incredible capacity to take the pen and rewrite that narrative, transforming it into a powerful story of resilience, growth, and, ultimately, redemption. Reframing your experience isn't about denying the pain or glossing over the difficulties; it's about choosing to focus on the strength you've gained and the positive transformation that has emerged.

Consider these examples of how you can consciously shift your perspective and rewrite your internal narrative:

- **Instead of "My life fell apart," try: "I was forced to rebuild , and I got to choose the blueprint."** This reframe emphasizes your agency and the opportunity you now have to create a life that truly aligns with your authentic self and your current desires. It shifts the focus from a passive sense of things falling apart to an active role in constructing something new and meaningful. ***Aha moment:*** *Recognizing that even in the face of upheaval, you have the power to take control and design your future.*

- **Instead of "I thought I was being buried, but I was being planted,"** this powerful metaphor suggests that the challenges you faced, while painful, were necessary for growth. Like a seed buried in the earth, you might have felt hidden and overwhelmed, but beneath the surface, roots were taking hold, preparing you for a new season of blossoming. ***Aha moment:*** *Understanding that even the most difficult experiences can be the foundation for significant personal growth and a new beginning.*

- **Instead of focusing on the negative aspects, consider: "The cracks let the light in."** This reframe highlights the idea that even in moments of brokenness, there is an opportunity for light, for new perspectives, and for a deeper understanding of yourself and the world around you to emerge. Your vulnerabilities can become pathways to greater empathy and connection. ***Aha moment:*** *Recognizing that imperfections and challenges can create openings for positive change and deeper understanding.*

Take some time to reflect on the negative narratives you might be telling yourself about your divorce. What are the phrases or statements that tend to dominate your thoughts? Now, try to brainstorm alternative ways of framing those experiences, focusing on your strength, your resilience, and the lessons you've learned. This conscious act of rewriting your narrative is a powerful step towards healing and empowerment.

Exercise: Letter to Your Past Self

Another powerful way to solidify your new narrative is to write a letter to your past self from your current perspective. Imagine you are writing to the version of yourself who was in the midst of the most difficult stages of your divorce journey.

- **"Dear You-in-the-Darkness,"** begin your letter with empathy and compassion for the pain you were experiencing.
- **"Here's what you can't see yet..."** In your letter, share the insights and wisdom you have gained since that time. What positive changes have occurred in your life? What strengths have you discovered within yourself? What would you want to reassure your past self about? Focus on the resilience you have demonstrated and the brighter future that awaits you.
- You might want to include messages of hope, validation, and encouragement. Remind your past

self that you are stronger than you think and that this difficult period will eventually lead to growth and new beginnings.

This exercise allows you to offer comfort and guidance to the part of yourself that endured the most pain while also reinforcing the positive transformation you have undergone. Aha moment: Experiencing a profound sense of closure and self-compassion by offering wisdom and reassurance to your past self from your current, stronger perspective.

Consider journaling regularly to explore and solidify your new narrative. By consciously choosing the story you tell yourself about your divorce, you are taking control of your healing journey and paving the way for a more empowered and hopeful future. Remember, you are the author of your own redemption story.

Paying It Forward; Your Hard-Won Wisdom

As you navigate further along your healing journey after divorce, you might begin to recognize the profound wisdom you've gained through this challenging experience. The path you've walked, though difficult, has equipped you with insights and understanding that can be incredibly valuable, not only for your own continued growth but also for supporting others who are just beginning or still struggling on a similar path. Your hard-won wisdom has the power to become a beacon of hope and a source of comfort for those who are feeling lost and overwhelmed.

Consider the unique qualities you now carry:

- **Empathy for others in crisis:** Having navigated the emotional complexities of divorce, you now possess a deeper capacity for empathy towards others who are facing similar lifequakes. You understand the raw pain, the uncertainty, and the myriad of emotions that can surface. This firsthand experience allows you to connect with others on a profound level, offering a genuine understanding that can be incredibly validating and comforting. *Aha moment: Recognizing the depth of empathy you now possess allows you to connect with others in a more meaningful way.*

- **The ability to say "I've been there" with authority:** There is immense power in sharing your lived experience. When you connect with someone who is going through a divorce and can honestly say, "I understand; I've been there," it carries a weight and authenticity that no textbook or well-meaning advice can replicate. Your ability to share your journey offers tangible proof that survival is possible and that healing does happen. *Aha moment: Understanding the unique value and authority that comes from your personal experience allows you to offer genuine reassurance and hope.*

- **Proof that survival is possible:** Your very presence, your resilience, and your continued journey towards healing serve as a powerful testament to the possibility of not just surviving divorce but ultimately thriving. You are a living example that even after profound heartbreak, it is possible to rebuild a fulfilling life. This silent proof can be incredibly inspiring to others who are currently in the midst of their own struggles. *Aha moment: Recognizing that your own journey and* *continued healing serve as a powerful source of hope and inspiration for others.*

Here are some ways you might choose to share your light and pay forward the wisdom you've gained:

- **Mentor someone newer to the journey:** If you feel ready, consider offering guidance and support to someone who is just beginning the divorce process. You can share practical advice, offer a listening ear, and provide reassurance based on your own experiences. Even a few conversations can make a significant difference in helping someone feel less alone and more hopeful.

- **Volunteer with divorce support organizations:** There are many organizations dedicated to helping individuals navigate the challenges of divorce. Consider volunteering your time or resources to these groups. You could lead support groups, share your story at events, or help with administrative tasks – any contribution can make a positive impact.

- **Simply live your truth, and your resilience inspires silently:** You don't necessarily need to actively seek out opportunities to share your wisdom. Simply living your life authentically, embracing your healing, and demonstrating your resilience can be a powerful source of inspiration for those around you. Your strength and your journey can silently encourage others who might be facing similar challenges. ***Aha moment:*** *Realizing that even your everyday life, lived with authenticity and resilience, can be a source of inspiration and hope for others.*

Sharing your hard-won wisdom can be a deeply fulfilling part of your own healing journey. It allows you to find meaning in your experiences and to connect with others in a way that is both supportive and empowering. By paying it forward, you not only help others navigate their challenges but also reinforce the strength and resilience you've cultivated within yourself. Your journey has equipped you with a unique and valuable gift – the gift of understanding and the power to offer hope.

The Ongoing Journey; Blessings Still Unfolding

The journey of healing and growth after divorce is not a sprint to the finish line but rather a continuous unfolding, a gentle blossoming that extends far beyond the initial stages. Just as a seed planted in fertile ground continues to grow and mature over time, the blessings and positive transformations that have emerged from your experience will also continue to reveal themselves in surprising and meaningful ways in the years to come. The gifts of this journey are not finite; they are often ongoing, subtle, and deeply personal.

Consider these ways in which the blessings might continue to unfold in your life:

- **Years from now, you'll notice a moment of gratitude for where life took you.** There might come a time, perhaps when you least expect it, when you look back at your journey and feel a profound sense of gratitude for the unexpected direction your life has taken. You might recognize that the path you are on now, though it may have been born from pain, has led you to experiences, connections, and a deeper understanding of yourself that wouldn't have been possible otherwise. This gratitude can arise from a place of strength, wisdom, and acceptance of your story in its entirety. *Aha moment: Envisioning a future where you can look back at this challenging time with a sense of gratitude for the growth and direction it ultimately provided.*

- **A challenge you handle with hard-won wisdom.** Life will inevitably continue to present its share of obstacles. However, the wisdom you have gained through navigating the complexities of divorce will serve as an invaluable resource in facing future challenges. You will likely find yourself approaching difficulties with greater resilience, a clearer understanding of your own needs and boundaries, and a deeper trust in your ability to overcome adversity. The lessons you've learned will become a quiet strength that guides you through whatever comes your way. *Aha moment: Recognizing that the wisdom gained from this experience will be a lasting asset, equipping you to navigate future challenges with greater confidence and grace.*

- **A joy that wouldn't have been possible before.** As you continue to build your new life, you might discover joys and opportunities that simply wouldn't have existed had your life path remained unchanged. This could involve new relationships, the pursuit of long-held dreams, a deeper connection with yourself, or a newfound appreciation for simple pleasures. These unexpected joys are beautiful reminders that life continues to offer wonderful possibilities, often in ways we cannot yet imagine. *Aha moment:*

Anticipating future joys and opportunities that are now open to you, possibilities that might not have emerged on your previous path.

"The story isn't over. The best blessings may still be unseen." This sentiment holds so much truth. Your journey of healing and growth is ongoing, and the full impact of this experience might not be apparent for many years to come. Remain open to the possibility that even more profound blessings and positive transformations are still waiting to unfold in your life. Cultivate a mindset of curiosity and anticipation for the good that is yet to come.

Continue to nurture your growth, embrace new experiences, and trust in the unfolding of your unique path. The wisdom, strength, and resilience you have gained are treasures that will continue to enrich your life in countless ways, revealing their beauty and value over time. The journey continues, and the best chapters, filled with unforeseen blessings, may still be waiting to be written.

Closing: The Light You Carry

You stand here today, dear reader, not as someone untouched by the storms of life but as someone who has weathered a significant tempest and emerged with strength and wisdom that only such an experience can forge. You are not unscarred but rather radiant in ways that only things broken and then carefully rebuilt can be. What once felt like a deep and painful wound has, over time, transformed into a wellspring of profound wisdom. What might have initially felt like abandonment has, through your own resilience and self-discovery, become the birthplace of your own autonomy and independence.

Consider these powerful truths as you move forward:

- **Scars as Wisdom:** The challenges you've faced and the pain you've endured have not left you diminished. Instead, they have etched lessons onto your heart, transforming your wounds into invaluable sources of wisdom and understanding.
- **Autonomy Born from Loss:** The initial feeling of being alone after divorce may have been difficult, but within that space, you have cultivated a deeper relationship with yourself, fostering a sense of independence and the freedom to shape your life on your own terms.
- **More Than Before:** You are not less for having loved and lost. In fact, you are more. Your capacity for empathy has deepened, your understanding of yourself has grown, and your resilience has been tested and proven. You carry within you a strength you might never have known otherwise.

These unseen blessings, these quiet gifts of growth and understanding, don't erase the pain you experienced. They don't diminish the significance of your loss. Instead, they transcend it, proving that even in life's cruelest seasons, grace exists. This grace wasn't present in spite of the storm but rather, in many ways, because of it.

Wherever your path leads you from here, please carry this truth with you: You are not less for having loved and lost. You are more, infinitely more, for having chosen to rise again, to heal, and to embrace the future with courage and hope.

And now, as we reach the close of this book, I want to express my sincere gratitude to you, dear reader. Thank you for being a part of this journey, for opening your heart and mind to these words, and for allowing me to walk alongside you, even in this small way, through a significant chapter of your life. It has been a privilege to share these reflections with you. May you continue to carry the light you have found within yourself, allowing it to illuminate your path towards a future filled with peace, joy, and the beautiful unfolding of all that you are becoming.

Reflection Questions: Gathering the Gifts

These final reflection questions are an invitation to actively gather the unseen blessings, the unexpected gifts of wisdom and strength that have emerged throughout your divorce journey. Take some quiet time to ponder each of these prompts, allowing your heart and mind to explore the depths of your experience. There are no right or wrong answers, only opportunities to recognize the profound growth and transformation you have undergone.

What's one strength I have now that I didn't before? Think deeply about the inner resources you've discovered within yourself as you navigated the challenges of divorce. What new strengths have you unearthed? Perhaps you've become more resilient in the face of adversity, more independent in your decision-making, or more attuned to your own needs and boundaries. Maybe you've developed a deeper sense of self-compassion or a newfound ability to trust your intuition. Identifying this specific strength allows you to acknowledge tangible personal growth and recognize the powerful ways in which you have evolved through this experience. Aha moment: Recognizing a concrete strength you've gained highlights your incredible resilience and personal evolution.

Who or what surprised me by becoming a blessing? Reflect on the unexpected sources of support, kindness, or positive influence that emerged during or after your divorce. Was there a friend, family member, or even a stranger who offered unexpected comfort or guidance? Did a particular experience, hobby, or newfound interest become a source of solace or joy? These unexpected blessings often appear when we need them most, reminding us that even in difficult times, there is still goodness and support to be found in the world around us. Acknowledging these surprising gifts can foster a sense of gratitude and connection. Aha moment: Appreciating the unexpected sources of blessing in your life can bring a sense of comfort and gratitude for the support you received.

If my highest self could thank this experience for one thing, what would it be? Imagine connecting with your wisest, most evolved self – the version of you that has gained the greatest perspective and understanding from this journey. If that highest self could express gratitude for one specific outcome or lesson from your divorce experience, what do you think it would be? Perhaps it would be thankful for the opportunity for profound self-discovery, the chance to redefine your life on your own terms, or the development of an unshakeable inner strength. This question encourages you to look beyond the immediate pain and consider the ultimate positive impact of this experience on your personal growth and evolution. Aha moment: Gaining a higher-level perspective on your journey and identifying a profound, positive takeaway that your wisest self would acknowledge with gratitude.

Journal Prompt:

"The unexpected gifts of this journey include..."

Take some time to write freely in your journal, listing the unexpected gifts and blessings that have emerged throughout your divorce experience. Don't censor yourself or judge your responses. Allow yourself to acknowledge even the smallest glimmers of positivity and growth. This could include newfound freedoms, stronger relationships, a clearer sense of purpose, or a deeper connection with yourself. Reflecting on these unexpected gifts can help you to appreciate the transformative power of your journey and to recognize the many ways in which you have grown and evolved. This practice can be a powerful reminder that even within challenging times, there are valuable lessons and blessings to be found.

Postscript: Finding Your Angels

As you gently close these pages, I want to take a moment to acknowledge the significant journey you've undertaken, not just through this book but through the profound experience of navigating divorce. Reaching this point is a testament to your strength, your resilience, and your unwavering commitment to healing and growth. You have bravely explored the complexities of loss, the importance of self-discovery, the solace of solitude, and the rekindling of hope. Remember that the path you've walked is deeply personal, and the insights you've gained are uniquely yours.

My most heartfelt wish in sharing my own story and the lessons I've learned is that you, too, will discover a path towards renewed happiness and a sense of profound peace. This happiness might not mirror the vision you once held, but perhaps it will be even richer, more authentic, and deeply aligned with the incredible person you are becoming. Embrace the freedom to redefine what joy means to you now. Actively seek out those moments that bring a smile to your face, nurture the connections that uplift your spirit, and allow yourself to pursue passions that ignite your soul. You are inherently worthy of a life filled with purpose and joy, and that possibility resides within you.

While the concept of complete closure might sometimes feel like a distant and perhaps unattainable ideal, I encourage you to strive for a sense of peace and acceptance regarding the chapters that have closed. Allow yourself the grace to acknowledge the past without letting it define your present or dictate your future. Release any lingering resentment or blame that weighs you down, and instead, focus your energy on building a life that feels authentic and fulfilling in this very moment. The freedom to create your own narrative lies within your grasp.

The journey of personal growth and the pursuit of happiness is not a destination to be reached but rather a continuous unfolding, a path with its own rhythm of light and shadow. There will still be times when challenges arise when you might feel moments of sadness or isolation. Please know that these are natural parts of life's tapestry. Remember the tools and insights we've explored together in this book – the power of reflection, the importance of self-compassion, and the courage to hope. These are resources you can draw upon whenever you need them, reminding you of your own strength and resilience.

You are a kindred spirit, navigating a human experience that, while deeply personal, connects us all through the threads of love, loss, and the enduring power of the heart. I have unwavering faith that you will continue to find your "angels" – those unexpected moments of grace, the supportive individuals who enter your life, and the quiet strength that resides within your own unshakable core. Face the future with the courage you have already demonstrated, armed with the wisdom you have so bravely earned.

And now, as we reach the end of our time together within these pages, I want to express my deepest and most sincere gratitude for allowing me to be a part of your journey. Thank you for opening your heart and mind to my story and for giving me the privilege of walking alongside you, even in this small way. It is my heartfelt hope that these words have offered you comfort, insight, and a renewed sense of possibility. May your path ahead be filled with peace, with joy, and with the unwavering knowledge that you are never truly alone.

With sincere love,

Eric

www.ingramcontent.com/pod-product-compliance
Lightning Source LLC
Chambersburg PA
CBHW061140120626
46546CB00005B/1869